EDUCATION

Practical Applications

Also in this series:

(Practical Applications)
Agriculture
Architecture
Art
Medicine
Religion
Science
Social and Political Science

(Esoteric)
Alchemy
Atlantis
Christian Rozenkreutz
The Druids
The Goddess
The Holy Grail

RUDOLF STEINER

EDUCATION
An Introductory Reader

Compiled with an introduction, commentary and notes by Christopher Clouder

Sophia Books

All translations revised by Christian von Arnim

Sophia Books
An imprint of Rudolf Steiner Press
Hillside House, The Square
Forest Row, RH18 5ES

www.rudolfsteinerpress.com

Published by Rudolf Steiner Press 2003

For earlier English publications of individual selections please
see pp. 208–10

The material by Rudolf Steiner was originally published in
German in various volumes of the 'GA' (*Rudolf Steiner
Gesamtausgabe* or Collected Works) by Rudolf Steiner Verlag,
Dornach. This authorized volume is published by permission of
the Rudolf Steiner Nachlassverwaltung, Dornach (for further
information see pp. 213–14)

A catalogue record for this book is available from the British
Library

ISBN 1 85584 118 5

Cover photograph by Aliki Sapountzi
Cover design by Andrew Morgan
Typeset by DP Photosetting, Aylesbury, Bucks.
Printed and bound in Great Britain by Cromwell Press Limited,
Trowbridge, Wilts.

Contents

Introduction

by Christopher Clouder

Although the texts in this book are the records of lectures given nearly a century ago, they still have a particular resonance for those concerned with education in the contemporary context. Rudolf Steiner's insights are as relevant to us as educators as they were to the people of his own time. His diagnosis of the failings of the educational system that was then practised and his emphasis on the real needs of the child are salutary reminders that in education we are faced with the continual struggle to improve, while at the same time responding to the new questions posed by social, economic and cultural changes. Yet in some respects we can find a constant. We struggle to realize principles and ideals and simultaneously assist children to find the capacities to live a life that involves compromises and an ability to adapt. Piaget stated that the true definition of intelligence is 'knowing what to do when you don't know what to do'. This is an intelligence that will increasingly be called upon in our twenty-first century world as the challenges facing us become more complex and demanding. Individual initiative and responsibility are essential in the creation of values and social harmony. 'The world is up for reinvention in so many ways. Creativity is born in chaos, what we do, why we do it, when we do it—these may be different and they could be better... Change comes from small initiatives that work, initiatives, which initiated, become the fashion. We cannot wait for great reasons from great people... It is up to us to light our own small fires in the darkness.'[1]

We are constantly being reminded that we live in a turbulent and changing world; our children will live in a world that we can barely conceive; and we can perceive that even the quality of childhood experience is a rapidly evolving one. With such a prognosis before us, education, in whatever context, cannot serve merely as a transmitter of accumulated knowledge but must take on formidable new tasks and be prepared to re-evaluate its methods, practices and intentions continually. Steiner's emphasis on this aspect of education as a force for renewal has a long West European pedigree dating back to Charlemagne in the ninth century CE. As King of the Franks and Emperor of the West, he set about cultural and political renewal of the state and a transformation of his people by implementing educational reforms and encouraging 'a new enthusiasm for human knowledge'.[2] This 'new enthusiasm' is a necessary concomitant for our intentions too and speaks clearly through all Steiner's 200 pedagogical lectures as well as his conversations with children, parents and teachers.

David Elkind, the eminent professor of child development at Tufts University, Massachusetts, recently wrote an article entitled 'Schooling the Postmodern Child', in which he states that Steiner was a forward-looking modern educational theorist whose insights are of great value in the post-modern educational debate. As we now increasingly live with the phenomenon of permeable families, rather than the more traditional and stable nuclear or extended family, Steiner education becomes a necessary area of stability and integration. Our society requires us to play many roles. In industry and commerce, for instance, familiar boundaries of work definition are less and less applicable and secure careers are no longer for life. We have to learn to coordinate our efforts in new ways. In many countries there is a shift in age structure with longer life expectancies and declining mortality rates as well as aging populations; female labour force participation has increased dramatically over the last two decades. Schools have taken on parental functions and early-years centres have to take responsibility for day care that was once seen as the province of the family. The international concept of 'early childhood education and care' brings together concepts and tasks that were previously discrete. The extended teacher-pupil relationship and the child's self-evident and uninterrupted belonging in the social grouping of a school class that is provided by Steiner education provides a place of secure interaction for the child. This sense of security and being respected and liked for who one is, as well as knowing that one's contribution to the class is welcomed, provides a healthy basis for self-confidence and later personal development

The approach to a curriculum that Steiner pioneered,

where the growth of knowledge and skills are viewed as an artistic and integrated totality, goes beyond the artificial subject divisions of a regulated timetable and prescriptive curriculum. Within a secure and predictable form children can find their own creative interrelationships. Elkind points out that the use of the narrative as a tool of understanding and comprehension, which is implicit in the Steiner method, takes into account the most fundamental way we, as humans, learn anything at all that goes beyond the boundaries of logic and reason. He concludes: 'Steiner's pedagogy is extremely innovative and particularly suited to the post-modern orientation and the permeable family. It remains for the rest of society to discover this educational programme that is so uniquely adapted to the needs and interests of the children growing up in today's post-modern world.'[3]

Already in 1898 Steiner was developing radical new ideas about new educational forms: 'Whether we have doubts about the veracity of what we convey or do not convey to the youth of today is of no importance. We convey these to young people with the implication: this is how we see the world; now look yourselves as to how the world appears to you. We have to awaken capacities and not offer convictions.'[4] His seminal lecture, which was given in response to numerous requests for him to address educational matters and which is entitled 'The Education of the Child in the Light of Spiritual Science', was given in Berlin in January 1907 and subsequently appeared as an essay. He refers to it later when speaking in Oxford: 'I was speaking on education there as one who disagrees with much in modern education, who would like to see this or the other treated more fundamentally...' It was this lecture that provided the basis of what was to come and lead to the approximately 900 schools now around the world, each of which was founded on individual initiative and endeavour. In this lecture, as he surveys the inner and outer development of the growing child, he reminds his audience that much of what he imparts remains to be fully worked out in the future: 'Of course these things can only be touched on here, but in the future, spiritual science will be called on to give the necessary indications in detail, which it is in a position to do. For it is not an empty abstraction, but a living body of facts that can provide guidelines for the conduct of life's realties.'[5] These guidelines are not an infinitely adaptable template but rather a resource for individual initiative and insight. Each school is autonomous and only the school community and those who have direct responsibility can make the necessary decisions that often require courage, self-development and creativity. Yet all share a common responsibility and wish to work together across all boundaries and hindrances. After more than 80 years of such experience, Steiner education is having an influence on the well-being of children that reaches beyond the confines of the schools and kindergartens themselves. This brings with it new challenges and paradoxes that confront all forward-looking educational practices and practitioners.

Looking forward is fraught with difficulties. Yet change is in the air and we have to come to terms with it and equip our children to do likewise. As it is put in the UNESCO report *Learning, The Treasure Within*: 'Education for pluralism is not just a safeguard against violence but an active principle for the enrichment of present-day societies. Between the extremes of abstract and over-simplifying universalism and the relativism which makes no higher demand going beyond the horizon of each particular culture, one needs to assert both the right to be different and receptiveness to universal values.'[6] For Steiner this was the ideal practice in every classroom in respecting the individuality and gifts of every child and forming a cohesive, appreciative and free society that embraces all humankind. Howard Gardner, whose scientific work led to the influential concept of multiple intelligences, comes to a similar conclusion. He expresses concern at the 'dis-ease' in our societies where success is often measured by values that are insufficient in that they ignore parts of the human spirit that should be respected. He affirms that education can equip us to make a difference. 'Our contributions depend on our rootedness in visions of the true, the beautiful and the good; our willingness to act upon these visions, individually and synergistically: our understanding of the changes as well as the constants of this world . . .'[7] Steiner also set the good, the beautiful and the true at the core of any meaningful curriculum and conscientious educational enterprise.

Steiner was remarkably percipient and there are many

currents of educational thought in our contemporary world that bear a marked resemblance to what he was saying and putting into practice in the first Waldorf school that was founded in Stuttgart in 1919. It came into being in the midst of the chaotic repercussions of the First World War. Europe and the world have experienced many convulsions since and the more we reflect on these human tragedies, and the more our biological and psychological knowledge of the human being grows, the more we can see the vital importance of those early years of our lives. Every teacher has to work with this because culture and knowledge cannot be divorced from values. Education is as much about how we are ourselves as the curriculum, school management, buildings, training and social acceptance. 'It is our task to let the future work in us ... If we are willing to focus our attention on the future by becoming aware of what is past and what is coming into being... Then another attitude arises in us concerning human destiny, an attitude that transcends egotism.'[8] He goes on to state that a teacher should not be permitted to instruct or educate 'without having acquired a concept of how the past and the future reach over into our culture. The Roman life of rights, the Greek spiritual substance, and the undefined rebel of the future that saves us.'[9] This is a statement of a man of the early twentieth century living in a Central European context who reaches out to something new born of his own spiritual insight, and simultaneously, as we shall see, a teacher with a global twenty-first century perspective.

These texts were originally given as lectures and not as pre-prepared papers, nor were they edited from stenographic records for later publication. Steiner was a consummate and popular lecturer whose audience could sometimes number thousands. He worked from the briefest of notes and his words were also created from a responsiveness and sensitivity to the listeners, as well as the historical, political and cultural context of his time. It is fascinating to see how his ideas and deep insights into education developed over time and he himself was prepared to change his perspective as his suggestions and ideals became realized in practice. As he categorically stated, all education is self-education.

1. A Social Basis for Education

Steiner gave three lectures on this theme in May and June 1919. During that time the first Waldorf school was being prepared and organized and at the same time the Versailles peace treaty was being negotiated. In April that year, Steiner had been invited by the managing director of the Waldorf Astoria cigarette factory in Stuttgart, Emil Molt, to speak to all his workers and colleagues about his vision of the renewal of a society devastated by the experiences of the war. These ideas went under the term 'the threefold social order' and were a diagnosis of the social failures that had led to such catastrophe, as well as representing radical proposals to ensure that such failures would never recur. These ideas were presented to the Versailles negotiators but ignored; however, they inspired many, including Emil Molt, who then resolved to pioneer an education based on them in the hope that future generations would know and act in a better way.

Steiner's April lecture was a call to action and an appeal against the status quo in which many were disadvantaged. He spoke of how the factory workers passed educational institutions each day on their way to work and how in these institutions the patterns of thought were propagated that the governing classes would then utilize. An unfair class structure was based on these educational and spiritual privileges and the time had now come when everybody had a right to an education that fulfilled them as human beings and gave them an equal chance for self-

*development. At a meeting on 23 April, the school was conceived
as the Free Waldorf School and Steiner then returned to develop
his ideas. This second of the series of lectures, like the others,
stresses the vital importance and the right of self-development
and of school education as provided in the basis for this in the
childhood years.*

*'Through the catastrophe of the World War which now, out-
wardly at least, lies behind us, history has wished to teach us a
lesson ... But the great misfortune of the present time is that
human beings have lost the capacity to learn. So, with the ear of
the spirit we may now hear resound through the world like a
battle-cry this call: learn how to learn!'[10]*

I do not propose today to follow up directly what I was
saying here last Sunday. On that occasion I tried, as far as
this was possible in mere outline, to show in a general
pedagogical and introductory way how we should conceive the organization of a life of spirit, of education,
independent of either the economic life or that of the state.
I also tried to show how, once this independence is
established, the various branches of instruction have to be
applied in a new way, in order to provide those things
which must reveal themselves to teachers and educators
as some kind of anthropological and pedagogical form or,
perhaps it is better to say, a kind of anthropologically
pedagogical activity. On the same occasion I remarked
that one essential in the future will be the training and
particularly the examination of a prospective teacher or

educator to discover whether his personality is fitted for the task.

I will reserve the direct continuation of these matters for a later occasion and try to pursue my main subject in quite another way. I shall try to put before you clearly how it is necessary for me to think out of the evolutionary forces of the age — and how today we should speak at teachers' conferences, for example, or at something of the sort, where people really desire to serve their times. At present it is a fact that, if we want to emerge from utter confusion and chaos, many things will have to be spoken of quite differently from how the present thinking habits prompt us to do.

Today even at teachers' conferences people talk — as can be proved by striking examples — along the old hackneyed lines. Yet it should be possible to introduce a really liberal education for the future, if only educators and teachers were able to rise to the level from which they could survey the very great tasks at present facing us, in so far as, out of the very nature of education and instruction, these tasks lend themselves to logical development. True, the manner in which I shall speak to you today will not be what I should like to hold up as a standard or even a pattern. But what I want to do is to indicate the angle from which we should speak to teachers so that they may themselves receive the impulse to get to work on an education which gives them freedom and room for manoeuvre. It is precisely those who do teaching who must rise to the level of the great and all-embracing tasks of the age; they must be first to gain insight into the nature of the forces concealed behind present world events; they must see which forces have to be recognized as coming from the past and therefore needing to be superseded, and which forces need to be specially cherished as having their roots in our present existence.

These matters must be looked at today culturally and politically in the best and most ideal sense if we are to create a foundation for the impulses which will have to exist in those who are teachers. Above all, people must become aware that at every stage of instruction and guidance our education has suffered impoverishment and the reasons for this must be understood. The principle reason is that education has lost its direct connection with life. Educationalists today talk of many things which have to do with method, above all the tremendous benefits that education will derive from state control. In an almost automatic way, it seems, they still speak of those benefits when in theory they have in part accepted the concept of the necessary threefold social organism. There has never been an age when thinking has been so automatic as it is now, and this is particularly evident where ideas on education are concerned. These ideas on education have suffered under something that up to now we have been unable to escape; we must, however, escape from it. There are indeed questions today that cannot find so easy a solution as the following: 'On the basis of past experience this or that will be possible.' Then doubt will immediately take possession of the hearts and minds of people. Today there are innumerable questions which will have to be answered by: 'Is it not imperative that something should happen if we are to extricate ourselves from confusion and chaos?' Here we are dealing with questions of will, where the often apparently justified intellectual doubt regarding the validity of experience can settle nothing. For experience has value only when worked upon in a suitable way by the will. Today there is much in the way of experience, though very little worked upon thus by the will. In the educational sphere itself a great deal is said against which, from the purely intellectual and scientific point of view, not much objection is to be made, and which from its own point of view is quite clever. But today it is important to understand the real issue—above all to understand how alien from real life our education has become.

I should here like again to refer to a personal incident. In Berlin about 23 years ago a society was formed concerned with college education. Its president was the astronomer Wilhelm Forster. I too belonged to this society. We had to hold a course of lectures, most of which were given on the assumption that all it was necessary to know were certain stereotyped things about dealing with the various branches of science, about grouping these into faculties, and so on. I tried—though at the time I was little understood—to draw attention to the fact that a college should be a department of life in general, that whoever wants to speak about college education ought to start with the question: 'From the standpoint of world history, what is our situation in life at present in all its different spheres, and what impulses have we to observe in these various spheres of life in order to let these impulses stream into the college, thus linking it with the common life?' When we work out such things, not in the abstract but concretely, countless points of view are revealed which, for example, help to reduce the time to be expended on any particular subject; and new ways of dealing with the various subjects are discovered. The moment any proposal is made for such a reduction simply out of the ideas with which education works today, everything collapses; the educational centres in question become mere institutions for training people who have no real connection with the world.

Now what are the intrinsic reasons, the underlying reasons, for all this? Whereas in recent times thinking on the lines of natural science has made such wonderful progress, this fine method of thinking, which on the one hand has come to look upon the human being as purely a being of nature, has—to speak the truth—cut off all knowledge of the real human being. We have spoken quite recently of the tremendous importance of this knowledge of the human being for the right kind of teacher—the knowledge that recognizes the real nature of living human beings, not in the formal way in which they are so often represented today but in accordance with their inner being, particularly in accordance with the evolution of that being. There is a symptom, to which I have often referred here, showing how dreadfully foreign the human being's real nature is to the modern educational movement. When something of this kind is said, it may perhaps be considered paradoxical; it must be said today, however, for it is of the utmost importance. The loss of any real knowledge of the human being has produced that dreary, barren effort that is a branch of what is called experimental psychology. I have no complaints against it as such, but the so-called intelligence tests are a horrible travesty of what is really beneficial in the sphere of education.

I have perhaps often described how, by certain physical contrivances, experiments are made with the avowed object of testing the memory, the understanding, of a human being, in order to register whether the particular person's memory and understanding are good or bad. In a purely mechanical manner, by giving part of a sentence and demanding its completion, or by some other device, the attempt is made to form an idea of the abilities of a growing human being. This is a symptom of how the direct relationship between people—which alone is profitable—is a forgotten factor in our culture. It is a symptom of something cheerless that has been allowed to develop; but today it is admired as being remarkable progress—this testing of intelligence, this offspring of what in modern universities are called psychological laboratories. Until people see how necessary it is to return to a direct intuitive knowledge of a person by studying the human being himself, particularly the growing human being, until we get rid of the unhappy gulf in this sphere between person and person, we shall never be able to

understand how to lay the foundations for an education
that is really alive and for a life of the spirit which is free.
We shall have to purge all our educational establishments
of this desire to experiment on the human being in order
to satisfy the educationalists. I consider experimental
psychology of value as providing the groundwork for a
reasonable psychology; in the form in which it has crept
into education and even into the courts, however, it is a
perversion of the sound development of the evolving
human being, between whom and his equally evolving
fellow there is no yawning chasm. We have brought
matters to such a pass that we have excluded everything
human from what we strive to achieve culturally; we must
retrace our steps and once again develop what belongs to
human beings. We have also to find the courage to make
an energetic stand against much of what in recent times
has aroused growing admiration as a great achievement;
otherwise we shall never make any progress. This
explains how those who leave college today with the
intention of teaching and proceed to educate people have
the most misguided conceptions about the real nature of
the human being. They fail to acquire a true conception
because the kind of superficiality has arisen in its place
that we can see in these intelligence tests. This will have to
be recognized as a symptom of decline. We must seek
within ourselves the capacity for judging the abilities of a
human being, since he is a person and we ourselves are
people. It must be understood that, because of this, every
other method is unsound, for it destroys the fullness of

what is immediately and vitally human — so necessary a factor in beneficial progress.

Now today these things are not recognized at all. It is of primary importance that they should be recognized if we are to progress. How often have these things been spoken of here! Sometimes they have even provoked a smile. But people have no notion that the reason for speaking of these things so frequently today is that they are an essential part of our life of spirit. There is nothing to be gained today by listening to what is said here as if it were a novel; the important thing is to learn to distinguish between what is merely perceived, observed, and what may contain within it the seed to action. The cumulative point of all the anthroposophical endeavours here is the development of the idea of the human being, the passing on of knowledge of the human being. It is this that we need. We need it because, from the very nature of the times, we have to overcome three forms of constraint, the remains of earlier days. First, the most ancient constraint which masquerades today in various forms — the constraint of the priesthood. We should make more progress in our study of the present situation were we today to recognize these disguises of certain obsolete facts and of the ideas and impulses unfortunately still living on in the thinking of the people in Europe, America and even in Asia — the modern disguises of the old priestly constraints.

As our second constraint we have something that develops later in man's historical evolution, also disguised in various ways today — the political constraint.

And thirdly, coming comparatively late, there is the economic constraint.

Human beings have to liberate themselves from these three constraining impulses; this is their task for the immediate present. They can get free today only if, to begin with, they clearly perceive the masks that in various ways disguise what is living in our midst, the masks that conceal the three constraining impulses among us.

Above all, teachers today must look to the level on which these things can be discussed, where, by means of the light gained from these things, we can illuminate contemporary evolution and thus become aware how one or the other of these constraints is lurking in some contemporary fact. Only when we find the courage to say: it is because teachers have isolated themselves, withdrawn into their schools, that such ill-judged ideas have been thought out as this testing of human efficiency by experiment — which is merely a symptom of much else ... But everywhere today, where either general or special educational methods are spoken of, we see the result of this withdrawal behind the school walls where teachers have been banished by the state; we see this remoteness from real life. None of the principle branches of life, namely, the spiritual, the rights or political and the economic, can develop fully at the present time — I say expressly at the present time, and particularly in this part of Europe — if these three branches do not stand each on their own ground. For the far West, America, and the far East it is rather different but, just because this is so, we ourselves must be aware of this. We shall have to think ultimately in concrete terms and not in abstract ones; otherwise, where location is concerned, we shall arrive at some theoretical Utopia for mankind throughout the entire earth, which is nonsense, or a kind of millennium in historical evolution—also nonsense. Thinking concretely in this sphere means thinking for a definite place and a definite time. We shall have something more to say about this today.

The attention of teachers must be directed towards the great world phenomena; they must be able to survey what is there in our present spiritual life, and what changes have to be made in this present life by bringing out of the growing human being something different from what has been cultivated in him of recent years. What has been cultivated latterly has, among those in educational circles who should have been active as teachers, led to terrible specialization. On occasions such as speech days, gatherings of scientists and other meetings of experts, we have often heard the praises of such specialization vociferously sung. Naturally it would be foolish on my part were I unable to see the necessity for this specialization in scientific spheres; but it needs to be balanced or we just create a gulf between one human being and another, no longer meeting our fellow human beings with understanding, but as specialists confronting them helplessly with other kinds of specialists. This gives us nothing on which to base our belief in a specialist but the fact that he bears the stamp of some existing body of knowledge. We have been very near bringing this specialization from the school into life. Whether the present vicissitudes will preserve us from the unhappy fate of having psychologists brought into the courts in addition to all the other experts, as many people wish, so that experiments can be conducted on criminals in the same way as they are conducted on our young people, this remains to be seen. I have less to say against the matter itself than against the way in which up to now it has been dealt with.

This is how things are under state control in the sphere of education, of school instruction.

Now after the brief period in which people talked of the inherent rights of the human being or, as they were then called, natural rights—no matter whether these were contestable or not—after this comparatively short time came the age when people began to be shy of discussing these natural rights. It was taken for granted that whoever did so was a dilettante. In other words, anyone was a dilettante who assumed the existence of something that established rights for a person as an individual human being; the only professional way was to speak of historical rights, that is, of those rights which had developed in the course of history. People did not have the courage to go into the question of the actual rights; and on that account they confined themselves to a study of the so-called historical ones. This especially is something that a teacher must know. Teachers must have their attention drawn, particularly during their conferences, to how in the course of the nineteenth century the concept of natural rights was lost, or lives on in rights today in disguise, and how a certain wavering, a certain inner doubt, has persisted in face of what is merely historical. Whoever is acquainted with the situation knows that the principle impulse today goes in the direction of historical rights, that people are at pains—to use Goethe's words—not to speak of inherent rights. In my lectures here I have frequently focused attention on how we must openly and honestly come to a final settlement in this matter. Hence we should not shrink from giving a true account of what has to be abolished, for nothing new can ever be set up unless there is a clear concept of what has impaired man's habits of thinking and perception.

It may well be said that our Central European culture is a particularly forcible example of how a really positive idea of the state has broken down. There was an attempt to build it up again in the nineteenth century. It foundered under the influence of the idea of purely historical rights which made their impulses felt without this being noticed by those concerned. Whereas people believed they were pursuing science in a way that was free from all prejudice, it really amounted to their pursuing it in the interest of the state or for some economic purpose. Not only in the way that science was conducted but also into its content, and especially into all that has become practical science, there has flowed what has come from the influence of the state. Hence today we have practically no national economy because a liberated thinking, established on its own basis, has been unable to develop. Hence, too, when laws relating to genuine political economy are mentioned, there is today an utter lack of understanding just where the most important laws of the economic life are concerned. We can see especially clearly the confusion into which education has been thrown — education on a grand scale — for it has no connection with life, it has withdrawn from life into the school room. A really living study of anything can never arise if we show merely what can be experienced outwardly, without showing the way in which it should be experienced. The one thing cultivated today, the worship of nothing but outward experience, leads simply to confusion, especially when it is undertaken conscientiously. We need the capacity to cultivate the inner impulses which lead us to the right experiences.

2. The Spirit of the Waldorf School

The speed with which the first school was set up and the teaching staff appointed for the opening on 7 September meant that a rapid training programme had to be put in place. Steiner was asking for a revolutionary approach that would have implications for generations to come. He embarked on a series of lectures for teachers as well as for those in the school community as a whole and, when the school had commenced, frequently addressed the pupils themselves. He emphasized that teaching is an art, and a fundamental foundation for the art of education is the perception of the child. Steiner imparted a new way of considering childhood as an integrated spiritual and physical process that could inform the teacher of what to teach and how to teach it if the adult was also prepared to observe and learn. From this perspective play becomes a significant factor as it evolves into other creative and social abilities in adult life. It cannot realistically be considered an element of childish behaviour divorced from learning and therefore needs respect and space within any educational process for young children. Steiner reminds us to be aware that academic training, then as now, can undermine this human faculty if it is not dealt with in an age and child-appropriate manner. A basis for a healthy and artistic education is about learning to integrate not segregate. Discernment and analysis need to be balanced with synthesis.

This, you see, is what we would like to develop in the Waldorf school faculty, to create in at least one place something for the future. We hope that the teachers will correctly recognize people and the relationship of people to modern culture, and that they will be inspired by this knowledge, by this feeling, to a will to work together with the child. Then true educational artists will emerge. Upbringing is never a science, it is an art. Teachers must be absorbed in it. They can only use what they know as a starting-point for the art of education.

We should not ramble on too much about the needs of teachers to have quite specific capabilities. These capabilities are more widespread than we think, only at present they are not very well developed. We need only the perseverance to develop them in the teachers in the right way, through a strong spiritual science. Then, we will find that what we call teaching ability is more wide-spread than we think.

You see, this is connected with something else again. Today, in theory, we are often warned against too much abstraction in instruction; but we still instinctively make these abstractions. It will concern those who see through these things that the plans and ideas for reform presently so common will make instruction more abstract than it is now. It will become worse in spite of all the beautiful ideas contained in these reform plans. If we study the stages of human development correctly, first the long stages up to the change of teeth and to sexual maturity, and then the shorter stages up to the development of a feeling of self and the sense of people separate from nature — if we study these epochs correctly, so that we do not tritely define them, but obtain an artistic, intuitive picture of them, then we can begin to understand how greatly the developing child is damaged when intellectual education is steered in the wrong direction. We should always emphasize the need to educate people as whole beings. But we can only bring up people as whole beings if we know their separate parts, including the soul and spirit, and understand how to put them together. We can never educate people as whole beings if in education we allow thinking, feeling and willing to interact chaotically. We can educate people as whole beings only if we intuitively know what the characteristics of thinking, of feeling, of willing are. Then, we can allow these powers of the human being to interact correctly in the soul and the spirit.

When people today discuss such things, they tend to fall into extremes. When people realize that intellect is too prominent, that our intellects are too strongly developed, they become enthusiastic about eradicating this imbalance, and say: 'Everything depends upon the development of will and feeling.' No, everything depends upon developing all three elements! We must develop people's intellect, feeling and will in the right way, so that they can understand how to let those three elements of life interact correctly. If we are to develop the intellectual element correctly, then during the elementary school period we must give children something that can grow with them, that can develop as a whole. Understand me correctly, particularly on this point, for it is an important point. Think about it. You develop in children until the age of 14 those ideas that you have carefully defined so the children know how they are to think them. But, just through the good definitions you have given them, you have often given them ideas that are quite rigid, that cannot grow with the person. People must grow from the age of 14 to 20, from the age of 20 to 25, and so forth, and at the same time their ideas must grow along with them. The ideas must be able to grow in parallel. If your definitions are too well formed, people grow, but their ideas do not grow with them. You guide intellectual development in the wrong direction. Then in cultural life, people will be unable to do anything except remember the ideas that you so carefully gave them. That would be wrong. Children's ideas should grow in parallel with their own development. Their ideas should grow so that what they learned at the age of 12 is, at the age of 35, as different from what it was when they first learned it as people in their physical bodies at the age of 35 are different from what they were at the age of 12. That is to say, in intellectual development we must not bring something well formed and dead, but teach something living, something that has life in it and can change. Thus, we will define as little as possible. If we want to bring ideas to a child, we will depict them from as many points of view as possible. We will not say: 'What is a lion? A lion is such and such.' Rather, we will depict a lion from many different points of view — we will instil living, moving ideas that will then live with the child. In this regard, modern education does much damage.

People must live through their earthly existence and often the ideas that we instil in them die and remain as soul corpses; they cannot live. We cannot get to the root of these things with the crude concepts developed by modern education. A very different spiritual impulse must imbue this education. That is something we strive for in the Waldorf school. We try to give education a new basis from which to consider such things psychologically. We are completely convinced that an understanding of human beings cannot arise out of the old principles, and that therefore these cannot be the principles of an education based upon psychology. We cannot form this psychology of the developing human with the methods that are so common today.

You see, when we can really, correctly observe such things, then we throw light on many secondary concepts that we hold to be very important today. We can easily understand them once we understand the main concepts. There is today, for instance, so much nonsense concerning the importance of play in the education of children. In considering the importance of play, we often forget the most important thing, namely, that if play is strongly regulated and children are made to direct their play towards a particular goal, then it is no longer play. The essence of play is that it is free. If, however, you make play really play, as is necessary for instruction, then you will not fall prey to the foolish expression, 'instruction should be just a game'. Then you will look more for the essential in the rhythm that comes into the life of the child when you allow play and work to alternate.

In training the mind and training feeling, we must give particular attention to the individual characteristics of the child. As teachers, we must be capable of forming the instruction so that the child does not simply receive something intellectual in the instruction, but enjoys the instruction in an aesthetic way. We cannot achieve this if the ideas appeal only to the intellect. We can do this if we, as teachers, relate to the children's feelings in such varied ways that we actually elicit the children's expectations of the subject, which we then fulfil. We can do this if we arouse hopes that, both large and small, we fulfil – if we develop every positive attribute of the children that can play a role in an aesthetic understanding of their surroundings. You can meet the child's aesthetic needs if you bring yourself into a correct relationship to the child's feelings, if you do not tritely 'sell' nature studies, as is done nowadays: 'Look, there is a mouse. The mouse runs. Was there ever a mouse at home? Have you ever seen a mousehole?' Of course, today instruction in nature study is not given in such extreme tastelessness, but in similar ways. People have no idea how much good taste, that is, the aesthetic experiencing of children, is damaged through what people nowadays call nature studies. We will develop taste only by steering the child's interest to large, inclusive views. For the proper unfolding of the mind, of feeling, taste must rule in instruction and in the schools. Thus, we can develop a certain instinct for the essentials in education.

To begin with, the intellect is the highest mental aspect in each of us; but if we develop it one-sidedly, without a concurrent development of feeling and will, then we also develop a tendency towards materialistic thinking. Although the intellect is our highest mental aspect during physical earthly life, intellect is directed towards materialism. Specifically, we should not believe that when we develop the intellect we also develop people spiritually. As paradoxical as that sounds, it is nevertheless true that we develop people's capacity to understand material things when we develop the intellect. By first tastefully, in an aesthetic way, developing sensitivity, the feelings, we can direct the human intellect towards the soul aspects. We can give children a foundation for directing the intellect towards the spirit only in so far as we practise a development of will, even if we develop it only as physical dexterity. That so few people today tend to direct their intellect towards the spirit can only be a consequence of the fact that the will was so incorrectly trained during childhood.

How do we as teachers learn to develop will in the proper way? I recently pointed out that we learn to do it by allowing children to be artistically active. As early as possible, we should not only allow children to hear music, to see drawings and paintings, but also allow them to participate. Besides mere instruction in reading and writing — yes, we must develop instruction in reading and writing from artistic activities, writing from drawing, and so forth — besides all this, basic artistic activities must take place early in education wherever possible. Otherwise, we will have weak-willed people. Directing young people towards what their later work will consist of comes in addition to this.

You see just how necessary it is in modern times that we come to a new understanding of humanity. This understanding can form the basis for a new way of educating, as much as this is possible within all the constraints that exist today. Because modern science does not comprehend these things, we must create something that leads in this direction through the Waldorf school.

It is urgently necessary that we do not allow ourselves to be deceived by much of what is said today. A week ago, I tried to explain the significance of the empty phrase for modern spiritual life. Empty phrases come into play particularly in educational reform plans. People feel good — and they believe that they are 'very pedagogical' — when they repeatedly admonish others to raise people, not robots. But those who say this must first know what a real human being is; otherwise this sentence becomes just an empty phrase. This is particularly so when the frequently asked question 'to what end should we educate children?' is answered by: 'to be happy and useful people'. Those who say this are referring to people who are useful in the way the speakers find useful and happy in the way the speakers mean happy.

It is especially important that we form a foundation that allows us to understand what human beings really are. However, this cannot be done with the old prejudices of our world view. It can only come from a new understanding of the world. A new form of education will not develop if we do not have the courage to come to a new scientific orientation. What we see most often today is people who want everything conceivable, but not what is necessary to arrive at a new orientation in understanding the world. We have been searching for this new orientation for years by means of spiritual science. If many people have distanced themselves from it, that is because they find it too uncomfortable or because they do not have the courage. But what we need for a real art of education can emerge only from a properly founded spiritual world view.

Think about the importance of what the teacher represents to the growing child. Basically, we people here on earth must continually learn from life if we are not to become set in one of the stages in our life. But, first we must learn to learn from life. Children must learn to learn from life in school so that, in later life, their dead ideas do not keep them from learning from life; so that, as adults, they do not become set in their ways. What keeps upsetting people today is that school gave them too little. Those who see through our deplorable social conditions know that they are largely connected with what I have just described. People do not have the inner hold on life that can come only when the right material is taught at the right time in school. Life remains closed if school does not give us the strength to open it. This is only possible if, in the early school years, the teacher is the representation of life itself. The peculiarity of youth is that the gulf still exists between people and life. We must bridge this gulf. The young senses, the young intellect, the young mind, the young will are not yet so formed that life can touch them in the right way. Children meet life through the teacher. The teacher stands before the child as, later, life stands there. Life must be concentrated in the teacher. Thus an intensive interest in life must imbue the teachers. Teachers must carry the life of the age in themselves. They must be conscious of this. Out of this consciousness can radiate what lively instruction and conduct should communicate to the pupils. To begin such a process, teachers must no longer be miserably confined to the realm of the school; they must feel themselves supported by the whole breadth of modern society and its interaction with the future, a future in which teachers in particular have the greatest interest. Under the present conditions and despite the present obstacles, we should try to do this in the school as well as it can be done by people who bring the necessary prerequisites from their current lives. We should not work out of any one-sided interest, out of a preference for this or that, but rather work on the basis of what speaks loudly and clearly to us as necessary for the development of present and future humanity. What in human developmental progress we see as necessary for our time should enter and strengthen instruction through the founding of the Waldorf school.

3. Educational Methods Based on Anthroposophy

As the school developed, more attention was paid to the practical life of the school based on the experiences there. In this lecture Steiner brings out the qualities of movements and their intrinsic value in education. Education should not be a matter of sitting behind desks and learning by rote. The importance of movement ➥ to neurological development and logical abilities is becoming more understood in neuro-biological and psychological research and these reaffirm Steiner's insights. The hand is as articulate as our mind. Our brain and hands can pull apart and divide (Latin articulare) *but can also be expressive and eloquent. The old wisdom that nimble fingers make nimble minds is finding scientific affirmation. Oliver Sacks puts the same point in a modern context: 'Sensation alone is not enough. It must be combined with emotion and action. Movement and sensation together become the antecedent of meaning.'[11] Steiner also explains why certain subjects should be taught at certain times so that there is a correlation between what the child experiences as his or her own inner and outer growth and what is experienced in the classroom and school. There is no fixed curriculum in the traditional sense but it is created in the relationship of teacher and child and their mutual perceptions. Although developed within Steiner schools, it is a method that is universally applicable.*

Yesterday, I sought to show how the philosophy and practice of an education based on anthroposophy rest on an intimate knowledge of human beings and hence also of growing human beings or children. I tried to show how a growing child can be regarded as a sort of 'time organism', so that we must always bear in mind that the activities of each succeeding year of a child's development occur against the background of that child's entire life. We can therefore plant something like soul and spiritual seeds in our children that will bear fruits of inner happiness and security in practical life situations for the rest of their earthly existences.

First, we looked at the period between birth and the change of teeth, when a child is a completely imitative being. We must realize that, during this first period of life, a young child is connected to its environment in an extremely intimate way. In a manner of speaking, every-thing that happens through the people around the young child, even their thoughts and feelings, affects the child in such a way that it grows into the happenings in its sur-rounding world by imitating them. This relationship—this connection to the surrounding world—has a kind of polar opposite in what happens during puberty.

Naturally, during the present age, with its materialistic overtones, there is much talk of the process of puberty. The phenomenon is usually viewed as an isolated event; however, to unprejudiced observation it must be seen rather as a consequence of a complete metamorphosis of the whole course of a person's life thus far. At this age, human beings develop not only their erotic feelings, coloured to a greater or lesser extent by soul and spiritual or physical aspects, but also their personal relationship to the external world. This begins with the forming of judgements that express themselves in strong sympathies and antipathies. Basically, it is only now that young people are placed fully within the world. Only at puberty do they attain the maturity to turn towards the world in such a way that independent thinking, feeling and judgement can live within them.

During the years between the change of teeth and puberty, a child's relationship to its teacher is based above all on the feeling of respect for the teacher's authority. Those important years can be regarded as lying between two polar opposites. One of them is the age of childhood when, without any subjective awareness, a child lives wholly within its outer surroundings. The other is the time of sexual maturity or puberty. At this time, adolescents as subjects differentiate themselves from the world — with all their newly awakened inwardness — by what could be called in the broadest sense sympathies and antipathies. In short, they distinguish themselves from the world by what we might call the various manifestations, or revelations, of love.

Between these two poles lies the lower school and, as teachers, it is our task to create a bridge from one pole to the other by means of education. During both stages — during early childhood as well as during puberty — the growing person finds a certain foothold in life, in childhood through union with the surrounding world and later through the feeling of being anchored within the self. The intervening years, encompassing the actual lower-school years, are the time when the growing child is in an unstable equilibrium, needing the support of the teacher and educator. Basically, during those years of primary education, the teacher stands as a representative of the entire world in the eyes of the child. That world is not one of mere arbitrary coincidence but rather the natural, lawful order in human development that is brought to life in what the teacher and educator means to the child. For the child, the teacher represents the whole world. Happy are those children who — before they must find a personal relation to the world by means of individual judgements, will impulses and feelings — receive the world through someone in whom the world is rightly reflected!

This is a deeply felt premise of the education that is to be based on anthroposophy. With this principle, we try to gain insight into the child's development, month by month, even week by week, in such intimate ways that we become able to read the curriculum and all our educational aims directly from the nature of the growing child. I could summarize this by saying: knowledge of the human being that is true and intimate also means knowledge of how and when — during which year and even during which month — to introduce the appropriate subject matter.

We must consider that until about the age of seven — and children should not really enter school before that age — a child lives entirely by imitation. Our young pupils are beings who strive with their will to be at one with their surroundings. This fact alone should preclude any appeal to the intellect, which depends on the soul's self-activity. Nor should we appeal to the child's personal feelings, which in any case are in complete sympathy with the environment. If we bear in mind that every response of such an imitative being bears a will character, we will realize how strongly the innate will nature meets us when we receive a child into school at the time of the second dentition.

Above all, then, we must begin by educating, instructing — training — the child's will. This in itself implies an emphasis on an artistic approach. For instance, when teaching writing we do not immediately introduce the letters of the alphabet in their present form because these have already become quite alienated from human nature. Rather, we begin by letting the children paint and draw, an activity that is a natural consequence and externalization of their will activities and that in turn leads to writing.

Proceeding in this way, a teacher notices in the children two different tendencies that should be given consideration. For whether we contribute to a child's future health or lack of health depends upon how we deal with these two tendencies. In relation to writing, we find two types of child. This becomes especially evident when we guide them towards writing through a kind of painting. One type of child learns to write in a way that always retains a quality of painting. This child writes 'with the eye', observing every line and working with an aesthetic feeling for the beauty of the form—a painterly quality lives in all his or her writing. The other type forms the letters on the paper more mechanically, with a certain compulsion. Even in writing lessons—often given for dubious pedagogical reasons, especially in the case of older persons who believe that they must improve their handwriting— the aim is usually to enable the participants to put their letters on paper with this mechanical kind of compulsion. This is how individual handwriting is developed. Just as people have their gestures, of which they are unaware, so too they have their handwriting, of which they are equally unaware. Those who write mechanically no longer experience an echo of their writing. Their gaze does not rest upon it with an aesthetic pleasure. They do not bring an artistic element of drawing into their writing.

/ Each child ought to be guided towards introducing this artistic element into handwriting. A child's eye should always rest on the piece of paper on which he or she is writing and so receive an impression of all that is being put into the writing. This will avoid writing under sheer inner mechanical compulsion, but will allow the child to experience an echo of his or her writing and the various letters. If we do this, we shall be cultivating a certain love in the child for what surrounds it—a sense of responsibility for its surroundings. Although this remark might sound improbable, it is nevertheless true. A caring attitude for whatever we do in life is a direct consequence of this way of learning to write—a method in which writing is a matter not only of manual dexterity but also for the eyes, for aesthetic seeing and willing.

We should not underestimate how such familiar things influence the whole of human life. Many persons who, later in life, appear lacking in a sense of responsibility — lacking in loving devotion to the surrounding world — would have been helped if they had been taught writing in the right way.

We must not overlook such intimate interconnections in education. Anthroposophy therefore seeks to shed light on all aspects of human nature — not just theoretically but lovingly. It tries to recognize the inherent soul and spiritual background of all external human traits and this allows it to add a completely practical dimension to the education of the young. If we remember to allow a child's forces of will to flow into such activities as writing, then learning to write — writing lessons — will eventually produce fruits of the kind I previously mentioned.

After writing, we proceed to reading lessons. Reading involves a child's life of feeling to a greater extent than writing and ought to develop from writing. Reading entails a greater element of observation, while writing is more a matter of active participation. But the starting-point in education should always be an appeal to the will element, to active participation, and not only to powers of observation.

Three steps should always be followed when teaching children aged from 7 to 14. First, the aim should be to involve the will, that is, the active participation of the pupils. Second, the aim is gradually to lead towards what becomes an attitude of observation. And only during the last phase of this period do we proceed to the third step, that of making of experiments, to experimentation.

Yesterday, I drew your attention to an important moment occurring between the ninth and tenth years. I pointed to the fact that much depends on a teacher's detecting the inner soul needs of each child at this critical stage and taking appropriate action. This moment in a child's development must be observed accurately. For only at this stage does the child begin to learn to differentiate its individual self from its surroundings. It does this in three ways—in feeling, in will activity and through the forming of judgements. The ability to distinguish between self and environment with full inner independence is achieved only at puberty.

Between the ninth and tenth years, a first harbinger of this separation from the surrounding world already begins to make itself felt. It is very important—just because we must support a child's being until puberty—that we recognize this moment and adapt our teaching accordingly. Up to this age, it is best not to expect children to distinguish themselves from their surroundings. We are always at a disadvantage when we as teachers introduce subjects—such as the study of nature—that require a certain objectivity, an inner distancing of the self from its surroundings, before a child is 9 or 10. The more teachers imbue the surrounding world with human qualities, the more they speak about it pictorially, and the more they employ an artistic approach, the better it is for the inner unfolding of their pupils' will natures. For, by becoming directly involved, these will natures are also thereby inwardly strengthened.

Everything musical helps deepen a child's will nature. After age 6 or 7, the element of music helps make a child more inward, more soulful. The will itself is strengthened by all pictorial and artistic activities—but only, of course, as long as they correspond to the child's age. Naturally, we cannot yet speak about plants, animals or even lifeless objects as something independent and separate. On the contrary, a child should feel that such things are an extension of its own being. Personification of outer objects and facts is right and appropriate during this time of a child's life.

We are wrong to believe that when we personify nature we are presenting a child with something untrue. Arguments of this kind have no validity. Our attitude should be: 'What must I bring to a child to liberate his or her life forces? What can I do so that what is within rises to the surface of life?' We can help this happen, above all, by being as lively as possible in our descriptions and stories of the surrounding world—if we make the whole surrounding world appear as if it issues from a human being's inner self. Everything introduced to the child at this age should be addressed to the child's whole being, not just to its head and nervous systems.

A false conception of human nature and an entirely misguided picture of human beings underlie current

attitudes towards education. We have a false understanding of the human being that overemphasizes the
nervous system. Rather, it is of prime importance that we
recognize a current flowing through the entire person
from below upwards — from the activity of the limbs and
from everything that follows from our relationship to the
external world — that impresses itself into the nervous
system and particularly into the brain. From this perspective, the anthroposophical study of the human being
is not being paradoxical when it maintains that, if a child
practises the appropriate movements at an earlier age, he
or she will develop intelligence, intellect, the power of
reasoning, the ability to discriminate, and so forth at a
later age. If we are asked why a particular child has not
developed a healthy ability to discriminate by the time he
or she is 13 or 14, why he or she makes such confused
judgements, we often have to answer: 'Because the child
was not encouraged to make the right kinds of physical
hand and foot movement in early childhood.'

The fact that eurythmy is a required subject in the
Waldorf curriculum shows that, from our point of view,
these remarks are justified. Eurythmy is an art of movement but it is also of great pedagogical value. Eurythmy is
truly a visible language. It is not like mime, nor is it a form
of dance. Rather, eurythmy originates in the perception of
tendencies towards movement in the human being that
may be observed — if I may borrow Goethe's expression —
with 'sensory-supersensory observation'. Those tendencies towards movement (I say 'tendencies' rather than

the actual movements themselves) are seen when human beings express themselves in speech, with the larynx and other speech organs performing the actual movements.

Those movements are transformed into moving air, which in turn becomes the carrier of sound and tone perceived by the ear. But there exist other inner tendencies or inclinations towards movement which proceed no further than the nascent state and yet can be studied by 'sensory-supersensory observation'. It is possible to study what is formed in a human being but never becomes an actual movement, being instead transformed, or metamorphosed, into movement of the larynx and the other speech organs.

In eurythmy, the movements are performed by one person or by groups whose movements produce an ordered, organic and visible form of speech, just as human speech organs produce audible speech or song. Each single movement—every detail of movement that is performed eurythmically—manifests such laws of the human organism as are found in speech or song.

This is why, in the Waldorf school, we witness again and again how—provided that it is taught properly—younger children in the first eight classes find their way into eurythmy, this new language, quite naturally. Just as, at this stage of development, a child's organism desires to move through imitation, so likewise is the child naturally inclined to reveal itself through the language of eurythmy. A sense of inner well-being depends on the possibility of the child's expressing itself through this medium. Older pupils develop the same inner response towards this visible language of eurythmy, only in a metamorphosed form, at a later stage. Indeed, we find that, just as eurythmy has been called forth from the inner order governing the human organism, it works back upon the human organization in a healthy manner.

For the moment, let us consider the human form. Let us take as an example the outer human form—although it would be equally possible to take the forms of inner organs—but let us for the moment take the human hand together with its arm. Can we really understand the form of the human hand and arm when they are in a position of rest? It would be an illusion to think that we could. We can understand the forms of the fingers, of the palm and of the arm only when we see them in movement. The resting form only makes sense when it begins to move. We could say that the hand at rest owes its form to the hand in movement and that the movements of the hand or arm must be as they are because of the form of the resting hand.

In the same way, one can summon forth from the whole human being the movements, like those connected with the vowels and consonants, that originate in the inner organization and are determined by the natural organization or form of the human being. Eurythmy has been created in harmony with the innate laws of the human form. A child experiences the change of the human form at rest into the form in movement—the meaningful transition into visible speech through eurythmy—with deep inner satisfaction and is thereby enabled to experience the inner life of its whole being. And this works back again in that the entire organism activates what is later transformed into intelligence in a way that should not be activated by anything else. If we try to develop a child's intelligence directly, we always introduce a more or less deadening or laming agent into its development. But, if we cultivate intelligence through the whole human being, then we proceed in a fundamentally healing manner. We endow the child with a form of intelligence that grows easily from the whole human being, whereas one-sided training of the intellect resembles something artificially grafted onto the organism.

By working back again on the spirit and the soul of children up to the ages of 9 and 10, eurythmy becomes an important educational aid. The same applies to later years when, between 9 and 10, a child learns to discriminate between the self and the external world. Here, however, one must be very careful about how such discrimination occurs. First, one must be careful not to introduce subject matter that predominantly activates a child's intellect and faculty of cognition.

From this point of view, before proceeding to mineralogy, physics and chemistry, it is good to introduce first animal and then plant study. Through the study of zoology and botany, children learn to discriminate between the inner and outer worlds in new and different ways. According to a given child's own nature, it might feel more akin to the animal world than to the plant kingdom. Pupils experience the plant world as a revelation of the outer world. On the other hand, with regard to the animal kingdom, children feel greater, more immediate rapport, inwardly sensing that there are similarities in many respects between animals and human beings. Teachers should definitely be aware of this when giving lessons in zoology and botany. Hence, when introducing botany, they should relate the plants to the earth as to a living organism. They should speak of the earth as a living organism. They should speak of it during the different seasons and of how it reveals itself by appropriate plant growth at different times of the year. In other words, they should introduce a temporal aspect into the study of plants.

The use of observational methods, while justifiable in other situations, can easily be disturbing if applied to botany and zoology. Generally speaking, far too little attention is given to the fact that the earth forms a unity with its plant growth. Again, you might find this paradoxical, but just as we can hardly study the organization of an animal's or a human being's hair separately — having rather to consider it in connection with the whole organism, as part of a whole — so we should also consider the earth as an organism and the plant world as part of it. If we introduce botany in this manner, a child, observing the plant kingdom, will differentiate its own being from the plant world in the right way.

On the other hand, the approach to animal study should be very different. Children feel a natural kinship, a 'soul bridge', with the animal world and this feeling of kinship should be taken into account. The opinions of older philosophers of nature are often smiled at today. But you will find all of the opinions of these older philosophers of nature in Goethe's way of looking at the animal world. According to the Goethean way, we look at the form of an animal and find, for instance, that in the form of the lion the development of the chest and the heart predominate, whereas in the case of other animals the digestive organs may predominate; in still other species, the teeth are especially developed, or the horns, and so on. We consider the various animal forms as expressions of single organs. In other words, we could say that there are head animals, chest animals and limb animals. Indeed, one could arrange the various animal forms according to even more subdivisions. This gives us the totality. Finally, taking all of the various animal forms together — synthesizing them in such a way that what predominates in a particular species regresses to fit itself back into a whole — we come to the form of a human being. From the point of view of outer form, therefore, the human being represents a synthesis of the entire animal world.

It is quite possible to call forth in the child a feeling for this synthesis of the entire animal kingdom in humanity. If we do this, we have achieved something very significant, for we have then allowed the child to relate both to the plant world and to the animal world in the right way. In the case of the animal world, the child can learn to see a human being spread across the entire animal kingdom and in the plant kingdom something that belongs organically to the whole earth. If, by giving individual examples, we can bring to life such a study of animals or plants at a deeper level, we respect at the same time how human beings should fit rightly into the world according to their inner nature. Then, just at the age when a child learns to differentiate itself from its surrounding world by beginning to discriminate between subject and object, she or he will grow into the world in the right way. Through the study of botany, we can succeed in separating the outer world from the inner life of a human being in the right way, and at the same time enable a child to build bridges into the world. Such bridges are essential if a right feeling for the world, if love for the world, is to develop. We can also do this by presenting the animal world to the child in the form of a picture of the human being unfolded or outspread. By doing so, we are following an organic, living path by allowing the child to find its proper relationship to living nature. Only when the twelfth year begins can we cultivate purely intellectual work and appeal to the powers of reasoning without harming a child's development.

When the curriculum that I have outlined today is followed, we begin by cultivating the life of the will. By presenting the child's relationship to the plant world and to the animal world in nature study, we begin the cultivation of the child's feeling life. The child then learns to relate to the plant and animal kingdoms not just theoretically. Indeed, the concepts gained from these lessons lay the foundations for a deeper relationship to the whole surrounding world. Something happens here that really touches the child's feeling, the child's psyche. And this is of immense importance; for, proceeding thus by engaging the child in the right kind of movement, and guiding and cultivating children's will forces and their lives of heart and soul up to almost the twelfth year, we can then find the transition to the actual cultivation of the intellect by introducing subject matter belonging to lifeless, inorganic nature.

Mineralogy, physics and chemistry should not be introduced before this age (the twelfth year). The only intellectual occupation not harmful during the earlier ages is arithmetic. This can be practised earlier because it is directly connected with an inner discipline and because it is neutral with regard to the cultivation of both will and heart or soul. Of course, it depends entirely on our knowing how to activate the child outwardly through the right kind of geometry and arithmetic during the age when the child is at the stage of authority.

Regarding the introduction of subjects belonging to inanimate nature, we should wait until approximately the twelfth year. Thus our ability to read in a child's nature what can and should be taught at each appropriate age is the whole point around which we form our curriculum.

If we introduce children to the external world in this way, we may be certain that we are preparing them for the practical sides of life also. Unfortunately, our present civilization does little to guide people into dealing with practical life. Rather, they are led into a routine life, the practical aspects of which consist in their being able to manipulate a few skills in a more or less mechanical fashion. Real love for practical work, love for working with one's hands, even if only crude and simple skills are required, is poorly cultivated by our present educational methods.

Yet, if we teach from insight into human nature, we will find a way to develop a genuine impulse to become practical people in those pupils who have reached puberty. For this reason, we introduce practical subjects in the Waldorf school as soon as our pupils reach puberty. We try to teach them crafts, which at the same time demand an artistic treatment.

The Waldorf school is a coeducational school and this policy has not thus far shown the slightest disadvantage from a pedagogical point of view. But what has also emerged is that boys love to do so-called girls' jobs — such as knitting, crocheting, and so on — and that it is precisely in these practical lessons that boys and girls in the Waldorf school work harmoniously together. You will perhaps forgive me for making a personal remark: men who as boys were taught to knit at school will know how much these skills have contributed to their ability to work with their heads and how their dexterity in using knitting needles, in threading darning needles, and so on has been transmuted into the development of logical thinking. This may sound peculiar to you, but it nevertheless belongs to one of the more hidden facts of life.

The origin of poor or faulty thinking is by no means always to be found in a person's innate intellectual capacities. What during a person's adult life is revealed as human intelligence must be traced back to the whole human being. Above all, we must realize that what is expressed through practical activities is intimately connected not only to the human head itself, but also to the way in which it has an effect on all that belongs generally to the cultivation of the sphere of the head.

If insight into the human being based on anthroposophy is to enter the field of education, it must guide the child towards a practical and realistic conception of life. Anthroposophy does not wish to lead anyone into a mystical 'cloud cuckoo land'. It does not wish to alienate people from practical life. On the contrary, it seeks to lead human beings into the fullness of practical life so that they really begin to love practical work. For instance, one cannot be a true philosopher in my opinion unless one is also capable of making a pair of shoes somehow or other, if the situation demands it, and unless one is capable of taking full part in all human activities. All specialization, however necessary it might be in life, can work in a healing way only if people are able to stand fully in life, at least to a certain degree. Naturally, not every adult can do this. Nevertheless, such is our aim in education, as I have taken the liberty of presenting it to you.

If we have thus guided our pupils from 'doing' to observing and, finally, to practical participation, which includes the making of scientific experiments — that is, if we have guided our pupils starting from training their will via observation permeated by human feeling to, finally, more intellectual work—if we have done all this, then we have followed a curriculum capable of planting seeds in their souls and spirits that will bear fruit throughout their lives. It is this wholeness of life that teachers must bear in mind at all times.

A great deal of thought has gone into finding the origin of morality. Ours is a time of abstraction; we philosophize about how human awareness of morality has found its way into life and where it is found in the individual and in the life of society. But so far, because our time is one of intellectualism and abstraction, we have not found its source in realistic terms. Let us seriously consider the idea that it is in the nature of the child, between second dentition and puberty, to surrender freely to the authority of a teacher who represents the whole world to the child. And let us accept that the child receives everything that enters its soul under the influence of this authority. If we do that, then we will adopt this line of thought in our education to give the child a picture of the educator and teacher as a living example of morality, one in which morality is personified. Listen carefully to what I say: teachers do not implant an ethical attitude by moralizing. To the child, they are morality personified, so that there is truly no need for them to moralize. Whatever they do will be considered right; whatever they refrain from doing will be considered wrong. Thus, in living contact between child and teacher, an entire system of sympathies and antipathies regarding matters of life will develop. Through those sympathies and antipathies, a right feeling for the dignity of human beings and for a proper involvement in life will develop. At this age, too, we can perhaps see emerging from the inner depths of the child's soul something that surfaces at times and needs only to be interpreted correctly.

This is how we can foresee the consequences of what we are implanting in childhood through education and school lessons. But we can also follow the consequences in social life. Social morality is a kind of plant that has its roots in the classroom in which children were taught between their seventh and fourteenth years. And just as a gardener will look at the soil of his garden, so society too should look at the 'soil of the school', for the ground for morality and goodness is to be found here.

Anthroposophy seeks to be knowledge of human beings that is able to satisfy both individual and social life. It wishes to fructify the various fields of life. Hence, it also wants to fructify theory and practice in education.

In only two lectures, it is impossible for me to give more than just a few suggestions. Anthroposophy will continue such work. What has been achieved so far regarding the foundations of education is only a modest beginning. In Dornach, at Christmas, I shall try to expand our anthroposophical education in a whole series of lectures, open to a wider international audience.[12] What I wished to show with the few guidelines that I have given here is that what matters most in anthroposophy is never a theory or a form of ideas leading to a certain conception of the world but practical life itself. This is certainly so in the field of education, although often it is unrecognized. Anthroposophy is often considered to be alienated from life. This, certainly, it does not want to be. Anthroposophy does not encourage adherents of spiritual knowledge to escape into 'cloud cuckoo land', thus estranging them from life. It strives for spiritual knowledge so that the spirit can be experienced in all its creativity, at work in all material existence. That the spirit is creative can be seen in the as yet small successes of the Free Waldorf School in Stuttgart. Teaching our pupils is by no means the only task of the Waldorf school. Many subsidiary activities are pursued there as well. Whenever I can be there, we have staff meetings. At those meetings, almost every pupil is discussed individually, not just from the point of view of making judgements but very much from the point of view of how and what we can learn from the individuality of each child. Wonderful results have emerged from such discussions.

For a long time now, I have wondered how a majority of boys or girls affects a class, for we have classes where boys are in the majority, others where girls predominate, and still others where the numbers of boys and girls are more or less balanced. It is never possible to predetermine, from personal contact with such classes, the effect of the relationships of boys to girls; imponderables play their part in the situation. But a class in which girls are in the majority is very different—neither better nor worse, of course, but all the same very different—from a class in which boys predominate. And again, a class in which the numbers are more evenly balanced has a very different character. However, something has come into being, especially through working in our meetings with the progress of our pupils — something that is already outwardly expressed in the way we write our school reports. This is what one could call 'the spirit of the Waldorf school'. When we talk about the school — I say this in all modesty — it is no longer enough to speak only about its 25 to 28 teachers; it is also possible to speak about the Waldorf school spirit.

This Waldorf school spirit spreads its life and existence beyond the school, right into the pupils' families. For I know how happy those families are to receive our annual reports and with what happiness our children take them home. I do not wish to tread on anyone's toes. Please forgive me if I mention a personal idiosyncrasy, but I have never been able to discriminate correctly among the various grades or marks that are given, say between B– and B or the difference between a 'nearly satisfactory' and a 'satisfactory'. In view of all the imponderables, I have always found it impossible to discern the differences that are indicated by such marks.

We do not make use of such marks in our reports. We simply describe the life of the pupil during the year, so that each report represents an individual effort by the teacher. We also include in each report a verse for the year that has been specially chosen for the individuality of the child in words with which she or he can live and in which he or she can find inner strength until the coming of a new verse at the end of the next school year. In that way, the report is an altogether individual event for the child. Proceeding thus, it is quite possible for the teacher to write some strong home truths into a report. The children will accept their mirror images, even if they are not altogether pleasing ones. In the Waldorf school, we have managed this not only through the relationship that has developed between teachers and pupils but also, above all, through something else that I could describe in further detail and that we have called 'the spirit of the Waldorf school'. This spirit is growing; it is an organic being. Naturally, I am speaking pictorially, but even such pictures represent a reality.

We are often told: 'Not all teachers can be perfect. In education one can have the best principles, but they founder on human weaknesses.' Yet if the living spirit of which I speak, which issues from anthroposophical knowledge of human beings, exists and if we can respond to it in the right way, then through it the human being can grow and mature. I hope that I am not saying too much when I tell you that the teachers in the Waldorf school have greatly matured through the spirit of the Waldorf school. They are aware of it; they can feel its presence among them. They are growing and developing under its guidance. They can feel how many of their individual gifts, which contribute to the life of the Waldorf school, become independent, blending into a homogeneous spirit, and how that spirit is working in all teachers and educators, planting seeds that can be of value for their pupils' whole lives in the ways that I have described. We can perceive it in various separate phenomena.

Naturally, we also have our share of less able children, and it has become necessary to separate some of them from their classmates. Hence, a very devoted teacher has organized a remedial class. Whenever a pupil is supposed to join the remedial class, his or her class teacher must endure a painful struggle, and no pupil is transferred to the remedial class except for the most urgent reasons. If we proceed merely by following a fixed scheme, many children would be sent into that special class, but a teacher often insists on keeping a child among his or her classmates, despite the great additional burdens that may be involved.

These are things that I mention not to boast but to characterize the situation. I would refrain from speaking about them were it not necessary to show that anthroposophy is capable of offering a sound educational basis on which to deal with the realities of life—an educational basis that leads to a spirit that will carry a human being without having to be supported, as is the case with an abstract form of spirit. This living spirit is what is needed in our decaying civilization. We should be able to consider each individual life problem within the context of life in general.

One problem, often called the most burning question of the day, is the so-called social question; it has drawn interest in the widest quarters. Apart from some positive aspects, this social question has also brought with it terrible misery — we only need to think of what is happening in Eastern Europe. It has many facets and one of these is doubtless that of education and teaching. One might even be justified in claiming that the social question, with all of its ramifications in the most varied areas of life, can hardly be put on a sound basis without dedication to the question of education from the social point of view, based on insight into human nature. Anthroposophy is anxious to deal honestly and seriously with all aspects of life and, above all, with education of the young.

Strangely enough, in our age of abstraction and intellectuality a certain concept has been completely lost with regard to spiritual and cultural life. But, if we go back to ancient Greece, we still find it. According to that concept, learning and teaching are at the same time healing and health-giving processes. In ancient Greece, people were still aware that teaching made human beings healthy, that what is given as soul and teaching content creates a process of healing. During the Greek stage of human evolution, teachers also felt themselves to be healers in the widest sense of the word. Certainly, times are always changing and the character of human development changes too. Concepts cannot remain unaltered. We cannot today return to the concept of a sinful humanity, and see in the child, too, a sinful member of humanity whom we must heal. From that point of view, we could see in education only a kind of higher, spiritual medicine. However, we see the situation more correctly when we realize that, depending upon how we affect a child by our education, we create health-giving or illness-inducing effects in the child's soul, which certainly affect its physical condition as well.

It is with this in mind—that human beings may develop in healthy ways in spirit, soul and body as far as this is possible within their given predispositions—that anthroposophical education and practice wishes to make its own contribution. Anthroposophy wishes to establish educational principles and methods that have a healing influence upon humanity, so that what we give to the child and what we do in the proximity of the child, though not amounting to medicine in a restricted sense, nevertheless become a way of turning human life in a healing direction—as regards both the individual and the body social.

4. The Child at Play

Play and playfulness lie at the heart of childhood and any form of education should take this into account if it seriously wishes to meet the needs of the child. As educational experiences often have a long-term effect and may not show their ramifications until much later, it has not been easy to show the effects of play deprivation. Yet recent research does show that those who have antisocial attitudes later in life and become frustrated in communication, therefore resorting to violent or antisocial means, have a history of play deprivation when young. 'Play becomes an experience of trust and spirit, of heart and body, of life and death, and of grace and grit. Literally my heart is at my fingertips. To put one's life into the hands of another is play.'[13] In Steiner kindergartens and early-year settings play is paramount and time for free play in a secure and homelike environment is part of the rhythm of each day.

But playfulness should not be just restricted to early years. Being at school should be an enjoyable experience for all concerned, neither just an obligation nor a mere legal requirement. Here humour plays a great role, and in his pedagogical lectures to teachers Steiner points out that unless one can bring a sense of humour into the classroom a sense of proportion can be lost and a useful tool in defusing confrontation or dealing with frustration is wasted. Education needs laughter and joy if the children are to thrive and face life's challenges with equanimity. A good school is where we can laugh together and it is not taken as a sign of disrespect or failure. Homo ludens *is a part of our creative self.*

If you view these matters in a comprehensive way, you will recognize that the entire human being has been taken into account in all that I have been trying to say about the art of education. This is the reason why we should introduce to a child aged 7 to 14 only what will be fruitful for his whole life. One needs to be aware of how an earlier stage of life affects a later one. I will go into further detail a little later. Only several years after a child has left school, when in fact he may have been an adult for many years, will it become evident what the school has given to him or neglected to do for him. And this will become apparent not in some general or abstract way but in quite concrete terms.

In this connection let us consider the child at play, especially the kind of play activities in which the youngest child is engaged between birth and the change of teeth. Such playing obviously is the outcome of the child's impulse to imitate. When playing, children imitate what they see the grown-ups do, but they do so in a different way. For their play is far removed from the purpose and usefulness with which the adults go about their business. Their play is only a symbolic imitation of the adults' activities and of no material consequence. The utilitarian and purposeful attitude to life is missing. The child experiences satisfaction in the activity that closely resembles the activity of the grown-up. We now need to investigate what it is that is really active in the child at play.

If we study this subject in order to recognize the true nature of human beings, and in order to be able to work towards their development in a practical way, we need to observe each single activity of the human soul, including that which flows into his physical organs. And this is not a simple matter.

Nevertheless, the study of play, taken in its widest sense, could be of real importance for the art of education. The child's play activity is connected with all kinds of things. At this point it might be helpful to recall the words of a great human spirit: 'The human being is a complete human being only as long as he plays; and he plays only as long as he is a complete human being.' These are the words that Schiller wrote in a letter after having read certain parts of Goethe's *Wilhelm Meister*. The free play of soul forces which Goethe unfolded in the artistic treatment of this work appeared to Schiller comparable only with the creativity of a playing child, but in this case transferred to the level of a grown-up. This is the fundamental theme running through Schiller's *Letters on the Aesthetic Education of Man*. It was Schiller's contention that an adult could never be a full human being because of the activities imposed upon him by ordinary life. Schiller argues that the human being either yields to the demands made upon him by his senses, which place him under a certain compulsion, or he follows logical necessity dictated by his reasoning, which again prevents him from acting as a free human individual. According to Schiller the human being is free only when he is engaged in artistic creativity and artistic thought. This line of argument is understandable in the case of an artistic nature such as Schiller's, but it is one-sided because there are so many other kinds of human experience that can take place in full inner freedom. The life situation in which Schiller sees the artist at work makes him experience the world of the spirit as if it were a natural and necessary part of life and, conversely, the world of the senses as if it were already belonging to the world of the spirit. This is certainly the case when we are enjoying art or when we are artistically creative. The artist works with sense-perceptible materials, but he does not do so for utilitarian purposes. He creates because he feels inspired by his ideas—using this word in its widest sense—but he does not follow abstract ideas dictated by logical necessity. When engaged in artistic creation, he is prompted by urges similar to those of hunger and thirst. He is satisfying entirely personal needs. Schiller felt that through artistic work the human being was able to achieve what the child in his creative play possessed as a natural gift—a gift which allowed him to take part in the world of the grown-up only in order to satisfy his needs. He also felt that the child was able to express himself through his play without having to serve any ulterior purpose.

Such were Schiller's reflections at the beginning of the nineteenth, and already at the end of the eighteenth century, ideas which can stimulate us to further thought. Yet it is not at all so easy to recognize the significance of play activity on psychological grounds. To do so, one would have to ask the question: does the play in which the child is engaged before the change of teeth have any significance for his entire life? Naturally one can analyse it according to Schiller, who felt inspired by Goethe's childlike creativity which bore the maturity of a grown-up genius. But it is equally possible to compare this play activity with a different soul process, namely, with what happens in a person's dreams. Here you will find meaningful analogies, but these refer only to the course which the child's play takes and to its inner connections. Just as a child puts together various objects in his play — whatever these may be — so do we weave together in our dreams not outer objects, of course, but thoughts and pictures. This does not apply to every type of dream, but certainly to a large number of them. When dreaming, we remain children for the whole of our lives, at least in certain fundamental respects. However, in order to reach a proper understanding, we must not be satisfied merely with comparing the activity of playing with the world of dreams. We have to ask ourselves: at what time in human life do the forces which are developing through play activity during the years before the second dentition bear fruit in a person's external life? When does he reap the fruits of what was developed through play activity in childhood? Usually people are inclined to look for the results of what was done at a certain period of life in the period immediately following. But here again, the science of the spirit has the task of showing that human life runs its course in definite rhythmic repetitions. In this respect human life follows a pattern which is similar to that of the plant. Out of the seed leaves develop in manifold shapes. Then follow sepals, petals, and so on. At the end of the plant cycle new seeds will sprout again. We find here, after a certain interval of time, a repetition of an earlier stage. The same kind of time pattern applies also to the course of a human life.

Nowadays, because of various methods of observation, one is led to believe that during the course of life each successive period is the result of the previous one. This, however, is not the case. If one observes the development of a person's life without preconceived notions, one will find that the results of play activity in childhood will manifest themselves only in the twenties. What a human being acquires between birth and the change of teeth through the activity of playing, and what is enacted before our eyes in such a dreamlike manner, are the forces of his yet unborn spirituality — unborn because they have not yet been absorbed by the physical body. I have already told you that the forces that have been building up the child's physical organism make themselves independent of the body after the change of teeth to become forces of thinking and ideation. During the change of teeth something is being withdrawn from the child's physical body, as it were. On the other hand, the forces flowing through the activities of a playing child have not yet anchored themselves to earthly life with all its practical tasks. They have not yet incarnated in the child's physical organization. This means that we are dealing here with two different kinds of forces. There are those working through the child's body, which after the change of teeth are transformed into the capacity of forming concepts that can be remembered. And there are other forces that are active within the child's soul and spiritual sphere, hovering lightly and etherically over the child, pervading his play activities in the same way in which dreams pervade our sleep during the whole of our lives. In the case of the child, the activity of these latter forces is developed not only during sleep, but also during the waking state, namely, while the child is playing. In this way they become an outer reality. However, what is being developed through this outer reality begins to recede after the seventh year. Just as the germinating forces in the plant recede during its leaf and petal formation to reappear only when the fruit is forming, so do the forces pervading the playing child reappear approximately in the twenty-first or twenty-second year, this time as powers of intellect which enable the human being to gather free and independent life experiences. And here I should like to ask you to make a real effort to grasp this transformation. Conscientiously observe and think about children. Try to understand the characteristic features of each child's play activities, especially those of his free play, up to the change of teeth. Form inner pictures of these children and then think quite hypothetically: the individual gesture as revealed in the child's play up to the second dentition will emerge again in the characteristic way in which, after the age of 20, he will form personal judgements. In other words, after the twentieth year different people vary with regard to their personal judgement in the same way in which, as children, they have differed in their play before the change of teeth.

If you think this through realistically, you will become aware of the immense responsibilities inherent in bringing up and educating children. You will begin to realize that what you are doing to the child will affect his future life well beyond the twenties. You will recognize that one needs to understand the entire course of life and not merely the age of childhood, if one wishes to build up a real art of education.

Between the change of teeth and puberty the child's playing assumes an entirely different character. Obviously this change occurs only gradually, but in order to grasp its significance in practical life one has to make clear distinctions. A perceptive observer will find that up to the seventh year the child's play bears a very individualistic character. When playing, the young child behaves somewhat like a hermit. He is contented to play in isolation. Certainly he will want help at times, demanding it in a terribly egoistic manner. However, during and after the second dentition a more sociable attitude begins to emerge. It is the time when children will happily play together. There are always exceptions to the rule, but on the whole, at this time of life, the child ceases to behave like a hermit in his play. Not only does he feel the desire to play with other children, but he also wants to cut a fine figure during such play. This wish to play an important part in social play is a typical feature of the period between the change of teeth and puberty. In countries with a militaristic tradition, boys love to play at soldiers. (I don't know whether Switzerland belongs to this group, neither do I wish to pass any judgement on the matter.) However, a companionable element enters into the children's play, giving them an opportunity for throwing their weight about, for most of them want to be generals at the very minimum. However, the characteristic feature of play remains preserved in so far as these childlike games are untouched by the realities and demands of daily life. Yet the strange thing is that what appears as the sociable element in play during the time between the change of teeth and puberty is already a kind of preparation for the next stage, for in puberty the faculty of individual judgement arises. It is a time when the adolescent emancipates himself from following authority, forming his own judgements and facing other people as an individual. This same element appears in play already during the preceding period, but free as yet from any other social ties. What is happening in play at this time is the first breaking away from authority.

Let us summarize: through the activity of playing during the first seven years the child gains forces which will embody themselves only in the twenty-first to twenty-second year, giving him the faculty of individual judgement based on intellectual capacity and life experience.

However, what is preparing itself during the play activities from the seventh year to puberty emerges earlier, namely, during the time from puberty to the twenty-first year. In this way a certain overlapping takes place. It is very interesting to realize that what we possess as faculties of intellect, of experiencing life and as faculties in the social realm we owe to the earliest years of our childhood, provided our play was guided rightly. And what emerges during the awkward and loutish stage of puberty we owe to the time between the change of teeth and puberty. In this way various phases of development are interrelated in human life.

And now let us look at what is happening in schools today merely because of a dependence on certain accepted prejudices. Thanks to some good instincts the situation has improved a little, but what is really needed is a radical change for the better. To give you one example: pupils are given too many definitions. As far as possible teachers should avoid giving children definitions, for these fetter the soul. Their concepts remain unchanged throughout life, introducing an element of death. Yet our task is to educate in such a way that what we instil into the souls of our children will remain alive. Let us suppose that a child in the ninth or eleventh year is forming concepts out of what he has learnt in his lessons. In the ninth year this may be the concept of a lion and in the eleventh to twelfth years the concept of Greek culture. This in itself is as it should be, but these concepts should not remain unaltered during life. It should never happen that a person, aged about 30, says: 'I have a certain concept of a lion or of ancient Greece, for I learnt it at school.' Such a state of affairs should not be allowed to continue. Just as everything else in us is growing and changing all the time, so whatever the teacher gives to his pupils should also grow and change; it should remain alive. Concepts such as those of a lion or of Greek culture, formed during the school years, should be so alive that at the age of 30 or 40 they will have progressed as life was progressing. To achieve this, we must give pupils characterizations instead of definitions. We should learn from the attitude with which we paint a picture or take a photograph. For when engaged in such activities we realize that we are able to look at our subject from one particular point of view only. In order to arrive at a comprehensive picture of a tree, we should have to take several photographs from various different angles.

We are too easily inclined to believe that a definition enables us 'to get hold of something'. But when working with our thoughts and concepts we should follow the example of taking photographs from different angles. We should feel convinced that instead of giving definitions, the only right way of proceeding is to characterize a living being or an object from many different points of view. The real purpose of a definition lies in our using it as a starting-point in order to establish a basis for an understanding between teacher and pupil. This is the fundamental task of definitions. Although such a remark may sound somewhat uncompromising, it nevertheless conveys the truth. Life does not love definitions. In our innermost selves we should feel that through the wrong use of a definition we turn a postulate into a dogma. It is very important for the teacher to realize this. Instead of saying: 'We call two things which cannot be in one and the same place at the same time impenetrable' – in this way consciously forming the concept of impenetrability before giving concrete examples of it – we should say: 'Bodies are impenetrable because they cannot be in one and the same place at the same time.' We must not turn postulates into dogmas. We are only right when stating that we call those bodies impenetrable which cannot be at one and the same place at the same time. We must be aware of the formative power of the soul. Therefore we must not let the child imagine that he will grasp the essential qualities of the triangle as seen in the external world before he has experienced the triangle inwardly.

This call for teachers to characterize rather than to define is based on the knowledge that what happens at one epoch of our lives will bear recognizable fruit only at a much later age, and that therefore we should transmit not dead but living concepts, thus giving the child a living apprehension of the world.

5. Teaching from a Foundation of Spiritual Insight and Education in the Light of Spiritual Science

Steiner's ideas on education were being formed well before the Waldorf school itself started. He had, so to speak, to wait until he was asked to put the idea into practice and the right individuals were there to carry it further. At this point Steiner was working from a theosophical standpoint from which, in the following years, he moved on and developed his ideas further as anthroposophy. These early lectures are a clear exposition of how he saw child development and he was convinced that education should be based on these observations, not on abstract theoretical considerations – that at certain times the child was ready for some things out of its own nature and at other times the same content and methods would be inappropriate. He here describes a fourfold aspect of the human being and how the interaction of these aspects undergoes transformation as we grow, and the implications for the child and childhood education. Although such a developmental picture has fallen out of favour with academic and other educational theorists, it is at present being referred to in a more positive vein and Steiner's work can stand alongside that of Piaget and Dewey in appreciating and explaining this quality of our humanness. Accordingly Dewey's statement 'Education is not a preparation for life, it is the process of life' gives a value to the school experience in itself. In the context of the classroom the teacher is facilitator of this development and creates the social order, aesthetic circumstances and learning content in which it can best happen.

I have often repudiated prejudices that foster the idea of theosophy as foreign to practical life. On the contrary, I have often spoken of how theosophy can lead us into practical life, because it teaches the laws that continuously form life around us. If you know only the laws of ordinary life, then you know only a small part of life. The major portion lies in those things hidden in life—that is, hidden from ordinary senses. People will soon recognize that to live better they must study the hidden worlds, since the materialistic approach leads to a crisis in nearly every area, but primarily in health care and education. The question arises of how we should educate people in the coming generations. Materialism leads to a crisis in all important social, political and cultural questions, since if we followed this path life would eventually be such that we would no longer know how to help ourselves. To illustrate this, I would like to say a few things of general interest about the question of education.

Those who consider education in a materialistic way will easily come to distorted conclusions. They will fail to consider the strong regularities of life and will therefore not consider the existence of clearly delineated periods of life. They simply cannot imagine, for example, why the period of childhood ending around age 6 to 8 years is so fundamentally different from the period beginning at approximately age 7 and continuing until puberty. If you have no idea of what happens to people during this time, you cannot imagine how important it is to observe it accurately. It is not of little importance to know what people are like during the first three periods of life. The first period proceeds until 6 to 8 years of age, the second until the age of 14 or 15, and the following period includes the next seven to eight years. We need to study these three stages in human life very accurately, not just externally but also from the standpoint of spiritual science, for spiritual science concerns itself with those worlds hidden from the ordinary senses.

You know that the human being does not consist of only the physical body; the human being also consists of an etheric body, which forms the basis of the physical and has a similar shape, and an astral body, which for the clairvoyant appears similar to a cloud, and in which the first two bodies are embedded. Within these, we find the vehicle of the I. We want to look more closely at these three bodies of the developing human being.

If you want to create a complete picture of the human being, then you must recall that a time exists before we can see people physically — that is, the time before birth when the child lives in the mother's body. On a purely physical level, you must differentiate clearly between the period before birth and the following periods, since the child could not live if born too early, if the child were to enter the ordinarily visible world too early. The child could not live because the sense organs, the means of interacting with the outer world, are not yet well enough developed. Those organs — the eyes, ears and everything needed to live in the physical world — develop during the time before birth while the child is still embraced by the mother's body. The child cannot come into contact with the physical world before its organs develop sufficiently within the protective mantle of another physical body. Birth occurs when a child is mature enough to encounter the physical environment without a protective mantle. We cannot say the same of the etheric and astral bodies. They are not nearly developed to the degree that they could come into direct contact with the physical surroundings.

During the period from birth until about 7 years of age, the etheric body undergoes a process similar to that undergone by the physical body before birth. Only at the end of that time can we say that the etheric body is 'born'. In the same way, the astral body is 'born' at the age of 14 or 15, and can then unfold its free and independent activity in the world.

You need to be aware that we may not place any particular demands on the etheric body until the age of 7, nor on the astral body until the age of 14. Exposing the baby's etheric body to the brutal demands of the world would be the same as exposing the foetus to the physical world in the fifth month of pregnancy, although we could not see it so readily. The same is true of exposing the astral body before the age of 14. Allow me to restate what I have just said. Until the age of 7, only the physical body is developed well enough to withstand the full effects of the world. Until that time, the etheric body is so occupied with its own development that it would be detrimental to try to affect it. Until then, we may, therefore, work only with the physical body. From the age of 7 until 14, we may take up the development of the etheric body, and only beginning with the age of 15 can we work upon the astral body.

To affect the human physical body means to provide the child with external stimuli. Such impressions act to develop the physical body, and for this reason we can hardly compensate for things neglected before the age of 7. Until the age of 7, the physical body exists in a state that requires external sense impressions to develop it. If a child's eye sees only beautiful things until the age of 7, the eye will develop so that it retains a feeling for beauty throughout life. Afterwards, the child's sense of beauty can no longer develop in the same way. What you say to a child and what you do until the age of 7 are much less important than the environment you create, what the child sees and hears. During this time, we must use external stimuli to support the child's inner growth. The child's free spirit creates a human figure from a piece of wood using only a couple of holes and some marks for the eyes, nose and mouth. If you give a child a beautiful doll, then the child becomes bound to it. The child's inner spirit clings to it and cannot develop its own activity; in this way, children almost entirely lose their imaginative powers.

It is essentially the same with all impressions of the

sense-perceptible world. Who you are in the presence of the child, what the child sees or hears, is important. The child will become a good person when surrounded by good people. Children imitate their surroundings. We must place particular value upon learning by example and the child's capacity to imitate. Thus, the correct thing to do is to act so the child can imitate as much as possible. In that sense, we must emphasize the child's physical development between the first and seventh year. During that period we cannot affect the higher bodies through educational methods, quite certainly not through conscious education. You affect these bodies through who you are in so far as they are not occupied with their own development. People can activate the child's good sense through their own good sense. Just as the mother's healthy body has a healthy effect upon the child's body, the teacher must attempt to be a well-rounded and self-contained person, to have high and good thoughts while in the presence of the child.

At the age of 7 the period begins when you can deliberately affect the etheric body. Here, two things connected with the development of the etheric body come into consideration—that is to say, habit and memory. The development of the etheric body depends on habits and remembrances. For this reason you should try to give children a firm foundation for life anchored in good habits. People who act differently every day, who lack a stable basis for their deeds, will later lack character. The task to fulfil between the ages of 7 and 14 is to create a basic set of habits and to stimulate memory development. Children need to learn upright habits and to have a rich store of memorized knowledge.

It is an erroneous belief of our materialistic times that very young children should learn to decide for themselves. On the contrary, we should do everything possible to hinder that. During this period of childhood, children should learn through authority. During the second seven-year period, people should instruct children and not teach through example. We form a strong memory, not by explaining all the 'whys' and 'wherefores', but through authority. We must surround children with people they can count on, people they can trust—people who can awaken in children a belief in the authority they hold. Only after this stage of life should we guide children into their capacity for judgement and independent reason. By freeing the child from the limitations imposed by authority, you rob the etheric body of the possibility of a well-founded development.

During the second seven-year period, it is best to give children examples and analogies, not proofs and conclusions. Conclusions affect the astral body, which is not yet free to receive them. You should tell children about great people, tell them in a way that great historical figures become examples for them. The same is true concerning questions of death and birth. If you can draw examples from nature, you will see what can be accomplished.

You could show children a caterpillar, how it spins a cocoon and afterwards a butterfly emerges. This is a wonderful example of how the child is created from the mother. You can accomplish a great deal if you use examples from nature.

It is just as important to teach children moral parables and not moral rules. We can clearly see this in a few sayings from Pythagoras. Instead of saying, 'If you want to accomplish something, do not concern yourself with things that you can see from the start will only be futile,' Pythagoras simply said, 'Don't strike at fire with your sword.' In another example, instead of saying, 'Don't meddle with things you know nothing about,' Pythagoras said, 'Keep your bean.' Along with the physical meaning, there is also a moral meaning here. In ancient Greece when people needed to make a decision they passed out black and white beans and then counted the number of beans of each colour returned. That is how they took votes. In this sense, instead of saying, 'Don't meddle in public affairs you know nothing about,' Pythagoras said simply, 'Keep your bean.'

In this way, you can appeal to the formative forces of imagination and not to those of the intellect. The more you use pictures, the more you affect the child. Goethe's mother could not have done anything better for him than to tell moral stories. She never preached at him. Sometimes she did not finish the story, so he made up the ending himself.

If we force children into critical thinking before the age of 14, it is particularly disadvantageous for them and forces them to create their own conclusions or lose the well-intended power of the surrounding persons of authority. It is very bad if children cannot look up to anyone. The etheric body becomes stunted, weak and shallow from lack of good examples on which to build. It is also particularly bad if children prematurely determine their religion and draw conclusions about the world. Children can do this only when their astral bodies can unfold freely. The more we protect children from premature judgemental and critical activities, the better it is for them. When the child's astral body has not yet become free, a wise teacher attempts to make reality comprehensible through the events themselves. Wise teachers do not demand a firm decision about religious confession, as is increasingly the common way of materialistic education.

The chaotic conditions between the religious confessions would quickly dissolve if we adhered to this more often. We should develop the capacity for judgement and reason as late as possible, only after the children's sense of individuality awakens—that is, when the astral body emerges. Before then children should not decide for themselves whom they believe but, instead, that should be a given. In the years that follow, the interrelationships of the sexes most strongly express individuality, that is, when one individual feels drawn to another.

You can see that if you study the three human bodies properly, you will find a practical basis for the proper education of children. Spiritual science is not impractical, not something living in the clouds; rather, spiritual science can provide the best guide for working with life.

That is precisely why we need a deepening of spiritual-scientific insight today, since without it humanity would reach a dead end. People today criticize the past, saying children were not called on at an early enough age to decide about God and the world, but in reality that was a healthy instinct. Now we must achieve that instinctive knowledge more consciously. The instinctive knowledge of earlier times has disappeared, and along with it a certain feeling of confidence about life's details. However, it is not possible to destroy humanity just like that. If we had strictly followed the dictates of materialism concerning education, medicine, jurisprudence, and so on, then human society would have fallen apart long ago. Yet not everything was destroyed, and some of the past still remains alive. We need the spiritual-scientific movement because materialism would, of necessity, lead people to a dead end.

Teachers who still have a feeling for the child's soul suffocate under a school bureaucracy and regulations that are only caricatures of what should actually exist, and they arise from a superstitious belief that teachers should deal only with the physical body. Blind religious belief is no protection against that either. It is important that people gain a sense of the spiritual and what exists beyond sense-perceptible life. Those who cling to educational formulas will never find the right things to do. They cling to traditional Church dogmas and don't want to know anything about spiritual development. But we seek spiritual development, since the answers to today's needs

must come from the spiritual worlds. The fruits of
materialism only cause illness in the human physical and
higher bodies. We cannot avoid a major crisis if people do
not engage in spiritual deepening.

The etheric body is the architect of the physical body.
The physical body crystallizes out of the etheric body
much as ice crystallizes out of water. We must therefore
regard everything that constitutes the physical aspect of a
person's being as having evolved from the etheric body.
Human beings have this body in common with every
being endowed with life — that is, with the vegetable and
animal kingdoms. In shape and size the etheric body
coincides with the physical body except for the lower part,
which differs in shape from the physical. The etheric body
in animals extends far beyond the physical body. For
anyone who has developed the spiritual faculties asleep in
every human being, there is nothing fantastic about this
description of the etheric body — in the same way that it is
not fantastic for a person who can see to describe colours
such as blue or red to a blind person.

The third element of a person's being, the astral body,
bears all kinds of emotions, lower as well as higher — joys
and sorrows, pleasure and pain, cravings and desires. Our
ordinary thoughts and will impulses are also contained in
the astral body. Like the etheric body, it becomes visible
when the higher senses are developed. The astral body
permeates the physical and etheric bodies and surrounds
humans like a kind of cloud. We have it in common with
the animal kingdom. It is in continuous movement,

mirroring every shade of feeling. But why the name astral?

The physical substances that make up the physical body connect it with the whole earth; similarly, the astral body is connected with the world of stars. The forces that permeate the astral body and condition a person's destiny and character were called astral by those who could look deeply into their mysterious connection with the astral world surrounding the earth.

The fourth element of a person's being, the power that enables one to say 'I', makes the human being the crown of creation. This name can only be applied to oneself; it expresses the fact that the soul's primordial divine spark is what speaks. We share the designations of everything else with others; a person's ear is accessible from outside, but not the name that refers to what is godlike in every individual human soul. That is why in Hebrew esoteric schools it was called the 'inexpressible name of God, Yahveh', and 'I Am the I Am'. Even the priest could utter it only with a shudder. The soul ascribes 'I am the I am' to itself.

The human physical body is related to the mineral kingdom, the etheric body to the vegetable kingdom and the astral body to the animal kingdom. Human beings have the 'I' in common with no other earthly being; the 'I' makes a human being the crown of creation. This fourfold entity has always been known in esoteric schools as the 'quaternity of human nature.'

These four bodies develop in each person in a particular

way, from childhood until old age. That is why, if we are to understand a person, we must always consider each human being individually. A person's characteristics are indicated already in the embryo. However, humans are not isolated beings but develop within a certain environment and thrive only when surrounded by all the beings of the universe. During embryonic life they must be enveloped by the maternal organism from which they become independent only when a certain stage of maturity is reached. During further development a child goes through more events of a similar nature. Just as the physical body during the embryonic stage must be enveloped by the maternal organism, so is it surrounded after birth by spiritual coverings related to spiritual realms. The child is enveloped by an etheric and an astral covering and reposes in them just as the child did in the womb before birth.

At the time of the change of teeth, the etheric covering loosens itself from the etheric body, as the physical covering did at physical birth. That means that the etheric body is born and becomes free in all directions. Until then an entity like itself was attached to it, and spiritual currents flowed from this entity through it just as physical currents flowed from the maternal covering through the child before birth. Thus, the child is born a second time when the etheric body is born. Meanwhile the astral body is still surrounded by its protective covering—a covering that strengthens and invigorates it until puberty. Then that also withdraws, the birth of the astral body takes place, and the child is born a third time.

The fact that a threefold birth occurs indicates that these three entities must be considered separately. While it is impossible for external light to reach and harm the eyes of the unborn child, it is not impossible — though certainly highly damaging to the soul — for foreign influences to be brought to bear on the etheric body before it has become completely independent. The same applies to the astral body before puberty. We should, according to spiritual science, avoid all education and training before the change of teeth, except what relates to the child's physical body; indeed, we should influence the etheric body as little as we influence the child's physical body before birth. However, just as the mother must be cared for because her health influences the development of the embryo, so one should now respect the inviolability of the etheric body for the benefit of the child's healthy development. This is important because, before the change of teeth, only the physical body is ready for the influences of the external world; all training should be restricted, therefore, to what concerns the physical body. Any external influence on the etheric body during this period is a violation of the laws that govern human development.

The human etheric body is different from that of the plant world because it becomes, in a person, the bearer of enduring traits such as habits, character, conscience, memory and temperament. The astral body is the seat of both the life of feelings already mentioned and the ability to discern, to judge.

These facts indicate the correct time to exert influence on the natural tendencies. In the period until the seventh year the child's bodily faculties develop; they become independent and self-contained. The same applies to the time between the seventh and the fourteenth year concerning habits, memory, temperament, and so on; the time between the fourteenth and the twentieth or twenty-second year is when the faculty of critical intellect develops, and a certain independence of the surrounding world is attained. All these things indicate that different principles of education are required in the various life periods. Special care must be exercised until the seventh year concerning everything that affects the physical body. This includes a great many things. It is a time when all the essential physical organs are gradually developing and the effect on the child's senses is of immense importance. It matters greatly what is seen, heard and absorbed in general. The faculty most prominent at this time is imitation. The Greek philosopher Aristotle remarked that human beings are the most imitative of all animals. This is especially true of a child before the change of teeth. Everything is imitated during this time, and since whatever enters a child through the senses as light and sound works formatively on the organs, it is most important that what surrounds the child should be beneficial.

At this age nothing is accomplished through admonition; commands and prohibitions have no effect at all. But setting an example is most important. What children see, what happens in their surroundings, they feel must be imitated. For example, parents were astonished to discover that their well-behaved child had taken money from a cashbox; greatly disturbed, they thought the child was inclined to steal. Questioning revealed that the child had simply imitated what his parents were seen to do every day.

It is important that the examples the child sees and imitates are of a kind that awaken inner forces. Exhortations have no effect, but the way a person acts in the child's presence matters greatly. It is far more important to refrain from doing what the child is not permitted to do than to forbid the child to imitate it.

It is vital, therefore, that during these years educators set an outstanding example, that they only do what is worthy of imitation. Education should consist of example and imitation. The truth of this is recognized when one gains insight into the nature of human beings, and it is confirmed by the results of education based upon it. Therefore, because the capacity to understand what things mean is a function of the etheric body, the child should not learn the significance of the letters of the alphabet before the change of teeth; before then, children should do no more than trace their form with paint.

Spiritual research makes all these subtleties understandable and sheds light even on the details of what should be done. Everything the child perceives — also in a moral sense — acts on the formation of its physical organs.

It does make a difference whether the child is surrounded by pain and sorrow or happiness and joy. Happiness and joy build sound organs and lay the foundation for future health. The opposite can create a disposition towards illness. Everything that surrounds the child should breathe an atmosphere of happiness and joy, including objects, colours of clothing, and wallpaper. The educator must ensure that this is the situation, while also considering the child's particular disposition.

A child who is inclined to be too earnest and too quiet will benefit from being surrounded by rather sombre, bluish, greenish colours, while a lively, over-active child should have yellow, reddish colours. This may seem like a contradiction but, in fact, through its inherent nature the sense of sight calls up the opposite colours. The bluish shades have an invigorating effect, while in the lively child the yellow-reddish shades call up the opposite colours.

So you can see that spiritual investigation sheds light even on practical details. The developing organs must be treated in ways that promote their health and inner forces. The child should not be given toys that are too finished and perfect, such as building blocks or perfect dolls. A doll made out of an old table napkin on which eyes, nose and mouth are indicated is far better. Any child will see such a home-made doll as a lady attired in beautiful finery. Why? Because it stirs the imagination, and that induces movement in the inner organs, and it produces a feeling of well-being in the child. Notice how such a child plays in a lively and interested way, throwing body and soul into what the imagination conjures up, while the child with the perfect doll just sits, unexcited and unamused. It has no possibility to add anything through imagination, so the inner organs are condemned to inactivity. Children have an extraordinarily sound instinct for what is good for them, as long as only the physical body has become free to interact with the external world, and as long as they are in the process of development. Children will indicate what is beneficial to them. However, if from an early stage this instinct is disregarded, it will disappear. Education should be based on happiness, on joy and a child's natural cravings. To practise asceticism at this age would be synonymous with undermining healthy development.

When the child approaches the seventh year and the baby teeth are gradually being replaced, the covering of the etheric body loosens and becomes free, as the physical body did at physical birth. Now the educator must provide everything that will promote the development of the etheric body. However, the teacher must guard against placing too much emphasis on developing the child's reason and intellect. Between the seventh and twelfth year, it is primarily a question of authority, confidence, trust and reverence. Character and habit are special qualities of the etheric body and must be fostered; but it is harmful to exert any influence on the reasoning faculty before puberty.

The development of the etheric body occurs in the period from the seventh until the sixteenth year in boys and until the fourteenth year in girls. It is important for the rest of a person's life that feelings of respect and veneration are fostered during this period. Such feelings can be awakened by means of information and narration—the lives of significant people can be depicted to children, not only from history but from their own circle, perhaps that of a revered relative. Awe and reverence are awakened in children that forbid them to harbour any critical thoughts or opposition against the venerated person. The children live in solemn expectation of the moment they will be permitted to meet this person. Finally the day arrives and the children stand before the door filled with awe and veneration; they turn the handle and enter the room that, for them, is a holy place. Such moments of veneration become forces of strength in later life. It is immensely important that the educator, the teacher, is at this time a respected authority for the child. A child's faith and confidence must be awakened—not through axioms, but through human beings.

People around the children, with whom they have contact, must be their ideals; children must also choose such ideals from history and literature. 'Everyone must choose the hero whose path to Olympus they will follow', is a true saying. The materialistic view that opposes authority and undervalues respect and reverence is totally wrong. It regards children as already self-reliant, but their healthy development is impaired if demands are made on the reasoning faculty before the astral body is born. At this time it is important that memory be developed. This is done best in a purely mechanical way. However, calculators should not be used; tables of multiplication, poems and so on should be committed to memory in a parrot-like fashion. It is simply materialistic prejudice to maintain that such things should be inwardly felt and understood at this age.

In previous times educators knew better. Between the ages of 1 and 7 all kinds of songs were sung to the children, such as the good old nursery rhymes and children's songs. Sense and meaning were not what mattered, but sound; the children were made aware of harmony and consonance, and we often find words inserted purely for the sake of their sound. Often the rhymes were meaningless. For example the German song: 'Fly beetle fly / your father is away / your mother is in Pommerland, Pommerland / fly beetle fly.' Incidentally, in the idiom of children Pommerland meant motherland. The expression stemmed from a time when it was still believed that human beings were spiritual beings and had come down to earth from a spiritual world. Pommerland was the land of spiritual origin. Yet it was not the meaning in such rhymes that was important, but the sound; thus many children's songs made no particular sense.

This is the age when memory, habit and character must be established, and this is achieved through authority. If the foundation of these traits is not laid during this period, it will result in behavioural shortcomings later. Precisely because axioms and rules of conduct have no place in education until the astral body is born, it is important that prepubescent children, if they are to be properly educated, can look up to authority. Children can sense a person's innermost being, and that is what they revere in those with authority. Whatever flows from the educator to children forms and develops conscience, character and even the temperament—their lasting dispositions. During these years allegories and symbols act formatively on the etheric body of children because such things manifest the world-spirit. Fairy-tales, legends and descriptions of heroes are a true blessing.

During this period, the etheric body must receive as much care as the physical body. During the earlier period happiness and joy influenced the forming of the organs; from 7 until 14—in the case of boys until 16—the emphasis must be on everything that promotes feelings of health and vigour. Hence the value of gymnastics. However, the desired effect will not be attained if the instructor aims at movements that solely benefit the physical body. It is important that the teacher should be able intuitively to enter into how children inwardly sense themselves, and to know in this way which movements will promote inner sensations of health, strength, well-being and pleasure in the bodily constitution. Only when gymnastic exercises induce feelings of growing strength are they of real value. It is not just the external aspect of the physical nature which benefits from correct gymnastic exercises; the way a person inwardly experiences the self also benefits.

Anything artistic has a strong influence on the etheric body as well as the astral body. Excellent vocal and instrumental music is particularly important, especially for the etheric body. And there should be many objects of true artistic beauty in the child's environment.

Most important of all is religious instruction. Images of things supersensible are deeply imprinted in the etheric body. The pupil's ability to have an opinion about religious faith is not important, but receiving descriptions of the supersensible, of what extends beyond the temporal, is. All religious subjects must be presented pictorially.

Great care must be taken that teaching is brought to life. Much is spoiled in the child if it is burdened with too much that is dull and lifeless. Whatever is taught in a lively, interesting manner benefits the child's etheric body. There should be much activity and doing, which has a quickening effect on the spirit. This is also true when it comes to play. The old kind of picture books have a stimulating effect because they contain figures that can be pulled by strings and suggest movement and inner life. Nothing has a more deadening effect on the child's spirit than putting together and fixing some structure, using finished geometrical shapes. That is why building blocks should not be used; the child should create everything from the beginning, learning to bring to life what is thus formed from the lifeless. Our materialistic age extinguishes life through mass-produced lifeless objects. Much dies in the young developing brain when the child has to do meaningless things like, for example, braiding. Talents are stifled and much that is unhealthy in our modern society can be traced back to the nursery. Inartistic, lifeless toys do not foster trust in spiritual life. A fundamental connection exists between today's lack of religious belief and the way young children are taught.

When puberty is reached, the astral covering falls away and the astral body becomes independent. With the awakening feelings for the opposite sex, the ability to judge, to form personal opinions, also awakens. Only now should the reasoning faculty be appealed to—the critical intellect's approval or disapproval. This is not to say that one can form independent judgements the moment this age is reached, let alone earlier. It is absurd for such young people to judge issues or to have a say in cultural life. A young person under the age of 20 has a still undeveloped astral body and can no more make sound judgements than a baby still in the womb can hear or see.

Each life period requires a corresponding influence. In the first, this is a model to be imitated; in the second an authority to emulate; the third requires rules of conduct, principles and axioms. The teacher is of paramount significance for the young person at this time—the personality that will guide students' eagerness for learning and their desire for independence in the right directions.

6. The Adolescent after the Fourteenth Year

Steiner often spoke of the pre-birth existence of the human being and that to grasp the educational task fully we had to take account of our spiritual and soul nature. Being born on earth had a spiritual intention behind it and we had taken on the tasks we face in life ourselves. To ignore what is immortal in a human being and what is non-physical would lead us to see only one side of the human condition. The child is more closely in contact with that world than an adult, but this contact diminishes as we learn to function and act in this world and develop capacities of logical thought and adult responsibilities. The adolescent stands at the crux of this change, and with the new ability to criticise, analyse and make adult judgements comes emotional turmoil and disorientation. As the young people acquire the ability to love in an adult fashion and to manage their own lives, so the school curriculum should provide a strength and inspiration for them. This means approaching the subjects taught in a new and creative way that is relevant to the adolescent and not trying to form them into merely functional citizens of the state. The young person should be able to find their own moral values and leave school able to make choices based on these values. In Steiner schools, as anywhere else, these ideals are difficult ones to live up to and it is vital that the teachers cooperate and work together as best they can, as colleagues in a common enterprise. The student will now come into contact with them as specialists in their particular subjects and will respect them according to how they are perceived and who they are, no longer because they happen to be in the vocation of a teacher.

During the second dentition, certain soul and spiritual forces in the child are released from working entirely in the organic sphere. They begin to assume an independent soul and spiritual character. Between the change of teeth and puberty the child develops a freer thinking, feeling and willing than was the case previously. No longer is it only an imitator, but through its natural feeling for authority it develops the degree of consciousness necessary for it to make contact with the world. This faith in the authority of a grown-up is essential, for the outer conditions of life are not sufficient in themselves to ensure the child's necessary contact with the world. The way in which one adult confronts another, whether by verbal or by other means of communication, is very different from the way in which a child meets an adult. The child simply needs the additional support that a sense of authority can give. As a consequence, more and more experiences from the child's waking state will enter its soul and spiritual life also during sleep. And to the same extent to which earthly experiences enter its sleeping state, replacing those of the spiritual world, the possibility is given to us teachers to reach the child between the change of teeth and puberty through our educational endeavours.

With the onset of puberty, an entirely new situation

arises, with the effect that fundamentally the emerging adolescent is a totally different being from what he was before sexual maturity. In order to characterize the situation, it may be useful to refer to what was spoken of at the end of yesterday's lecture. Up to the change of teeth, it is normal for a child to live entirely within the physical body. However, if this state is extended beyond its normal time — and in later life such a situation would no longer represent normal conditions — the consequences will be a markedly melancholic temperament. During childhood it is natural to have the kind of relationship between the soul-spiritual and physical organization that is characteristic of an adult melancholic. We must always bear in mind that what is right and good for one stage of life becomes abnormal for another. During the second dentition certain soul and spiritual forces are freed from their previous organic activities and they flow into what I have called the body of formative forces, or the etheric body. This element of the human being is entirely linked to the external world and it is right for the child to live in it during the time between the change of teeth and puberty. If already before the change of teeth there was an excess of these etheric forces, that is, if the child has lived too much in its etheric covering before the second dentition, the outcome is a markedly phlegmatic temperament. However, it is quite possible for a child to have a normal and balanced relationship with the etheric body and this is absolutely essential between the seventh and the fourteenth year, that is, between the change of teeth and puberty. Again, if this condition is carried over too far into later life, a decidedly phlegmatic temperament will develop in the grown-up.

The next element of the human being which under normal circumstances gains its independent existence in puberty and which yesterday I called the astral body — the element of the human being that lives beyond space and time — is the real birthplace of the sanguine temperament. And if during the time between the change of teeth and puberty a child draws too much upon what should come into its own only when sexual maturity is reached, the sanguine temperament comes into being. Only with the arrival of puberty does the growing human being become inwardly mature for sanguinity. Thus everything in life has its right or normal period of time. The various abnormalities come about if that which is normal for one particular time of life is pushed into another period of life. If you can survey life from this viewpoint, you learn to understand the human being in depth. So, what is actually happening during the time of sexual maturity? Our considerations of the last few days have already shed some light on it. We have seen how after the change of teeth the child is still working inwardly with those forces which, to a certain degree, have become emancipated soul and spiritual forces. During the subsequent stages the child incarnates via the system of breathing and blood circulation to where in the tendons the muscles are attached to the bones. It incarnates from within outwards towards the human periphery, and at the time of sexual maturity the young adolescent breaks through into the external world. Only then does she or he fully stand in the world.

This dramatic development makes it imperative for the teacher to approach the adolescent, who has passed through sexual maturity, quite differently from the way in which he had dealt with him or her prior to this event. For, fundamentally, the previous processes involving the emancipated soul and spiritual forces before puberty had as yet nothing to do with sex in its own realm. True, boys or girls show a definite predisposition towards their sexes, but this cannot be considered as actual sexuality. Sexuality only develops after the breakthrough into the external world, when a new relationship with the outer world has been established. But then at this particular time something is happening within the realm of the adolescent's soul and bodily nature which is not unlike what happened previously during the second dentition. During the change of teeth, forces were liberated to become actively engaged in the child's thinking, feeling and willing, forces which were directed more towards the memory. The powers of memory were then released. Now, at puberty, something else becomes available for free activity in the soul realm. These are powers which previously had entered the rhythms of breathing and which subsequently were striving to introduce rhythmical qualities also into the muscular system and even into the bones. This rhythmical element now becomes transmuted into the adolescent's receptiveness for all that belongs to the realm of creative ideas, for all that belongs to the imagination.

Fundamentally speaking, genuine powers of imagination are born only during puberty, for they can come into their own only after the astral body has been born. It is this same astral body which exists beyond time and space and which links together past, present and future according to its own principles, as we can experience it in our dreams.

What is it that the adolescent brings with him when he 'breaks through' into the external world via his skeletal system? It is what originally he brought down with him from pre-earthly existence and what, gradually, became interwoven with his whole inner being. And now, with the onset of sexual maturity, the adolescent is being cast out of the spiritual world, as it were. Without exaggerating, one can really put it that strongly, for it represents the actual truth; with the coming of puberty the young human being is cast out from the living world of the spirit, and thrown into the external world which he or she can perceive only by means of the physical and etheric body. And though the adolescent is not at all aware of what is going on inside him, subconsciously it plays a part which is all the more intensive. Subconsciously or semi-consciously, it makes the adolescent compare the world he has now entered with the world that he formerly had within himself. Previously he had not experienced the spiritual world consciously, but nevertheless he had found it possible to live in harmony with it. His inner being felt attuned to it and ready to cooperate freely with the soul and spiritual realm. But now, in these changed conditions, the external world no longer offers such possibilities to him. It presents all kinds of obstacles which, in themselves, create the wish to overcome them. This, in turn, gives rise to the tumultuous relationship between the adolescent and the surrounding world, lasting from the fourteenth or fifteenth year till the early twenties.

This inner upheaval is bound to come and it is well for the teacher to be aware of it already during the previous years. There may be people of an unduly sensitive nature who believe that it would be better to save teenagers from such inner turmoil, only to find that they have made themselves their greatest enemy. It would be quite wrong to try to spare them this tempestuous time of life. It is far better to plan ahead in one's educational aims so that what has been done with the pre-puberty child can now come to the help and support of the adolescent's soul and spiritual struggles.

The teacher must be clear that with the arrival of puberty an altogether different being emerges, born out of a new relationship with the world. It is no good appealing to the pupil's previous sense of authority, for now he demands to know reasons for whatever he is expected to do. The teacher must get into the habit of approaching the young man or woman rationally. For example, if the adolescent who has been led by the spiritual world into this earthly world becomes rebellious because this new world is so different from what he had expected, the adult must try to show him—and this without any pedantry— that everything he meets in the world has had a prehistory. He must get the adolescent to see that present conditions are the consequences of what had gone on before. One must act the part of the expert who really understands why things have come to be as they are. From now on, one will accomplish nothing by way of authority. Now one has to be able to convince the adolescent through the sheer weight of one's indisputable knowledge and expertise and by giving him watertight reasons for everything one does or expects of him. If, at this stage, the pupil cannot see sound reasons in all the content given to him, if conditions in the world appear to make no sense to him, he will begin to doubt the rightness of his previous life. He will feel himself in opposition with what he had experienced during those years, which apparently merely led him into these present unacceptable outer conditions. And if during his inner turmoil he cannot find contact with people who are able to reassure him, at least to a certain extent, that there are good reasons for what is happening in the world, then the inner stress may become intolerable to the extent that the adolescent breaks down altogether. For this newly emerged astral body is not of this world. The young person has been cast out of the astral world and he is willing to place himself into this earthly world only if he feels convinced of its rightful existence.

You will completely misunderstand what I have been describing if you think that the adolescent is at all aware of what is thus going on within him. During his ordinary day-consciousness it rises up from the unconscious in dim feelings. It surges up through blunted will impulses. It comes to expression in the disappointment of apparently unattainable ideals, in frustrated desires and perhaps also in a certain inner dullness towards what presents itself out there in the unreasonable happenings of the world.

If during this stage education is to be effective at all — and this indeed must be the case for any youngster willing to learn — then the teaching content must be transmitted in the appropriate form. It must also be a preparation for the years to come, up to the early twenties or even later in life. Having suffered the wounds inflicted by life and having paid back in his own coinage, the young person of 15 to 21 or 22 eventually will have to find his way back again into the world from which he had been cast out during puberty. (The duration of this period varies, especially so during our chaotic times, which tend to prolong it even further into adult life.) The young person must feel accepted again; he must be able to make new contact with the spiritual world, for without it life is not possible. However, should he feel any coercion coming from those in authority, this new link will lose all meaning and value for life.

If we are aware of these difficulties already well before the arrival of puberty, we will make good use of the child's inborn longing for authority in order to bring it to the stage when there is no longer any need for an authoritarian approach. And this stage should coincide with the coming of sexual maturity. But by then the educator must always be ready and able to give convincing reasons for everything he wishes his pupil to do.

Seen from a wider, spiritual perspective, we can thus observe the magnificent metamorphosis which takes place in the human being during the period of sexual maturity.

It is of the greatest importance to realize that the whole question of sex becomes a reality only during puberty, when the adolescent enters the external world in the way I have described it. Naturally, since everything in life is relative, this too has to be taken as a relative truth. Nevertheless, one has to recognize that up to the stage of sexual maturity the child lives more as a general human being, and that an experience of the world differentiated according to whether one lives as a man or woman only begins with the onset of puberty. This realization, which in our generally intellectual and naturalistic civilization cannot be taken for granted, will allow people who without prejudice are striving for a knowledge of the human being a real insight into the relationship between the sexes. It also helps them to understand the problem regarding the position of women in society, not only during our present times but also in the future.

One will only be able to understand fully the statement that up to the age of sexual maturity the child retains a more general human character, as yet undivided into sexes, if one can appreciate the tremendous metamorphosis that takes place in the male organism when the voice breaks — to mention just one example. Other similar processes occur also in the female organism, only in a different area. The human voice with its ability to moderate and to form sounds and tones is a manifestation of the human being's general human nature. It is born out of the soul and spiritual substance which works upon the child up to puberty. Changes of pitch and register, on the other hand, which occur as the voice breaks are the result of external influences. They are forced upon the adolescent from outside, as it were. They are the means by which he places himself into the outer world with his innermost being. It is not only a case of the soft parts in the larynx relating themselves more strongly to the bones, but a slight ossification of the larynx itself takes place which, fundamentally, amounts to a withdrawal of the larynx from the purely human inner nature into a more earthly existence.

This stepping out into the world should really be seen in a much wider context than is usually the case. The capacity to love which awakens at this time is usually directly linked in people's minds to sexual attraction. But this is by no means the whole story. The power to love, born during sexual maturity, embraces everything within the adolescent's entire compass. Love between the sexes is but one specific and limited aspect of love in the world. Only by seeing human love in this light can one understand it correctly, and then one also understands its task in the world.

What really happens in a human being during the process of sexual maturity? Prior to this stage, as a child, his relationship to the world was one where he first imitated the surroundings and was then subsequently subject to the power of authority. Outer influences were working upon him for at that time his inner being mainly represented what he had brought down with him from pre-earthly life. Humanity as a whole had to work upon him from without, first through the principle of imitation and then through authority. But now, at puberty, having found his own way into humanity and no longer depending on its outer support to the same extent that a pre-puberty child does, there rises up in him a new feeling and an entirely new appraisal of humankind as a whole. It is this new experience of humankind which represents the spiritual counterpart to the physical faculty of reproduction. Physically he becomes able to procreate. Spiritually he becomes capable of experiencing mankind as a totality.

During this new stage, the polarity between men and women becomes very marked. Only through a real understanding of the other sex by means of social intercourse, also in the realm of soul and spirit, is it possible for human potential to come to some kind of realization on earth. Both men and women fully represent humankind, but each in a differentiated way. The woman sees in humanity a gift of the metaphysical worlds. Fundamentally, she sees humanity as the result of a divine outpouring. Unconsciously and in the depths of her soul she bears a picture of humankind which acts as her standard of values, and she evaluates and assesses humankind according to this standard. If these remarks are not generally accepted today, it is due to the fact that our present culture shows all the signs of a male-dominated society.

7. Science, Art, Religion and Morality

Steiner's lectures in England, where he gave three cycles on education in Oxford, Ilkley and Torquay, as well as lectures in London and Stratford-upon-Avon, all have a pragmatism and straightforwardness about them. This introductory one in Ilkley is a helpful introduction to 'anthroposophy' and its relationship to the schools and their educational practice. He insisted the school is a place where the children 'should unfold their whole being' – holistic or integrated education in our contemporary parlance. But it would never a be place where anthroposophy as such is taught. During the conference Steiner remarked that every time he passed the book table he shuddered because of the number of books on 'anthroposophy' that were there. In his view it was a term that should be changed every week because in it lurked the danger that it would come to represent a fixed way of perceiving the world, and therefore a dogma, or that it would suggest that a particular way of viewing the world was taught in the schools. Neither is the case. He used the term to describe an 'international medium of understanding' and path of self-development that had practical applications in many areas of human activity, including education. For the teacher it is a way of gaining insight and skills so the lessons can be imaginative, rich in content, enjoyable and full of enthusiasm. For Steiner teachers themselves, it provides a source of inspiration and cohesion whereby the school communities can work together both within the school and worldwide. However, the schools are not anthroposophical institutions and what is developed within them is a method that is universally applicable. To underline this approach, the talks in Ilkley were for the public and reported in full in the local paper. Given the misunderstanding and conflicts in our world, his approach to a religious attitude that can foster reverence and is not divisive is as timely now as it was then.

My first words must be a reply to the kind welcome given by Miss Beverley to Frau Doctor Steiner and myself, and I can assure you that we deeply appreciate the invitation to give this course of lectures. My essential task will be to show what anthroposophy has to say on the subject of education and to describe the attempt already made in the Waldorf school in Stuttgart to apply the educational principles arising out of anthroposophy. We gladly accepted the invitation to come to the north of England and it gives me deep satisfaction to speak on a subject which I consider so important, the more so as I am also speaking to those who have arranged this course and are not listening to lectures on this subject from this perspective for the first time. I hope, therefore, that more lies behind this conference than only the resolve of those who organized it, but that it may be taken as evidence that our previous activities are bearing fruit in current world strivings.

English friends of anthroposophy were with us at a conference held at Christmas two years ago when the

Goetheanum—since taken from us by fire—was still standing. The conference was arranged by Mrs Mackenzie, the author of a skilled book on Hegel's educational principles, and the sympathetic appreciation expressed there makes one hope that it is not, after all, so very difficult to find understanding that transcends the limits of nationality. What I myself said about education at the conference was not, of course, based on the more intellectualistic philosophy of Hegel but on anthroposophy, the nature of which is wholly spiritual. But again it was Mrs Mackenzie who found that something fruitful for education could be won out of anthroposophy which, while taking full account of Hegel, passes beyond his intellectuality into the spiritual.

Then I spoke about our educational principles and their practical application a second time last year, in the old university town of Oxford. And perhaps I am justified in thinking that those lectures, which amongst other things dealt with how education is related to the social life, may have induced quite a number of English people concerned with education to visit our Waldorf school in Stuttgart. It was a great joy to welcome them there in the classrooms of the school, amid the work of educating and teaching going on in those rooms, and we were delighted to hear that they were satisfied with our work and were following it with interest. The idea of holding this summer course on education seems to have arisen during that visit. Its roots, therefore, may be said to lie in previous activities and this very fact gives one the right confidence and the right courage as we embark upon the present lectures. Courage and confidence are necessary when one has to speak of matters still so unfamiliar to the spiritual life of today and in the face of such strong opposition as comes from many quarters. More especially are they necessary when one attempts to explain principles that approach in a creative sense the greatest artistic achievement of the cosmos — the human being himself.

Those who visited us will have realized the significant way in which Waldorf education gets to grips with the deepest threads of modern life. The educational methods applied here can really no longer be described by the word 'pedagogy' — a valuable word which the Greeks learnt from Plato and the Platonists, who devoted themselves so sincerely to all educational questions. Pedagogy is, indeed, no longer an apt term today, for it shows straightaway the one-sidedness of its ideals, and those who visited the Waldorf school will have realized this from the first. It is not, of course, unusual today to find boys and girls educated together in the same classes and taught in the same way, and I merely mention this to show you that in this respect, too, the methods of the Waldorf school are in line with recent developments.

What does the word 'pedagogy' suggest? The 'pedagogue' is a teacher of boys. This shows us at once that in ancient Greece education was very one-sided. One half of humanity was excluded from serious education. To the Greeks, the boy alone was man and the girl must stay in the background when it was a question of serious education. The pedagogue was a teacher of boys, concerned only with that sex.

In our times, the presence of girl-pupils in schools is no longer unusual, although it does, indeed, involve a radical change from customs which are by no means very ancient. Another feature of the Waldorf school, however, will even today have something strange about it for many people. Not only are boys and girls equal as pupils, but also on the teaching staff no distinction of sex is made, no distinction at any rate in principle, even up to the highest classes. Universal human considerations laid it upon us to get rid of this one-sidedness. We had first to give up all that was contained in the old term 'pedagogy' if we wanted to establish an education in accordance with modern conditions. That is only one aspect of an educational one-sidedness implied by the name. Speaking in the broadest sense, it must be said that until recently nothing at all was known in education of the human being as such. Indeed, many one-sided views have been held in the educational world—not only that of the separation of the sexes.

When the pupils had passed through the years of schooling according to the old principles, did a human being as such emerge? Never! Today, however, human-kind is preparing to seek for the human being, for the pure, undimmed, undifferentiated human. That this had to be sought can be seen from the way in which the Waldorf school was formed.

The first idea was to provide an education for children whose parents were working in the Waldorf-Astoria factory, and as the director was a member of the Anthroposophical Society, he asked me to arrange this education. I myself could do it only on the basis of anthroposophy. And so, in the first place, the Waldorf school arose as a school for human beings as such, created, we might say, out of the working class. It was only 'anthroposophical' in the sense that the man who first had the idea of the school happened to be an anthroposophist. Here, then, we have an educational institution arising on a social basis that seeks to found the whole spirit and method of its teaching upon anthroposophy. It was not, however, in the remotest sense a question of founding an 'anthroposophical' school. On the contrary, we hold that because anthroposophy is at all times able to take a background role it is able to set up a school on universally human principles and not upon the basis of social rank, philosophical conceptions or any other special interest.

This may well have occurred to those who visited the Waldorf school; and it is evident in every single thing that is done there. It may also have led to the invitation to give these present lectures. And in this introductory lecture, when I have not yet started to speak about education, let me cordially thank all those who have arranged this summer course. I would also thank them for having arranged performances of eurythmy, which has already become such an integral part of anthroposophy. At the very beginning let me express this hope. A summer course has brought us together. We have gathered together in a beautiful spot in the north of England, far away from the busy life of the winter months. You have given u time of summer recreation to hear of subjects that w ⌐ an important part in the life of the future, and the time must come when the spirit uniting us now for a fortnight during the summer holidays will inspire all our winter work. I cannot adequately express my gratitude for the fact that you have dedicated your holidays to the study of ideas significant for the future. Just as sincerely as I thank you for this now, so do I trust that the spirit of our summer course may be carried on into the winter months — for only so can this course bear real fruit.

Allow me to refer to the impressive words of Miss Macmillan yesterday, in which a deep social and educational impulse found expression, and which in a sense bore witness that profound moral impulses must be sought if human civilization as a whole is to make further progress in education. When we allow the significance of such an impulse to work deeply in our hearts, we are led to the most fundamental problems in modern spiritual life — problems connected with the forms assumed by our culture and civilization in the course of human history. We are living in an age when certain spheres of culture, though standing alongside one another to a certain extent, are yet separated from one another. In the first place, we have everything that human beings can learn of the world through knowledge — communicated, for the most part, by the intellect alone. Then there is the sphere of art, where human beings try to give expression to profound inner experiences, imitating with their human powers a divine creative activity. Again we have the religious strivings, the religious longings of human beings, wherein they seek to unite the roots of their own existence with those of the universe. Lastly, we try to bring forth from within ourselves impulses that place us as moral beings in the civilized life of the world. In effect we confront four branches of culture: knowledge, art, religion, morality. But the course of human evolution has brought it about that these four branches are developing separately, and we no longer realize their common roots. It is of no value to criticize these conditions; they are necessities, but they must be understood. Today, therefore, we will remind ourselves of the beginnings of civilization. There was an ancient period in human evolution when science, art, religion and the moral life were one. It was an age when the intellect had not yet developed its present abstract nature and when human beings sought to solve the riddles of existence by a kind of picture-consciousness. Mighty pictures stood there before their souls — pictures which in decadent form have since come down to us as myths and sagas. Originally they proceeded from actual experience and knowledge of the spiritual content of the universe. There was indeed an age when in this direct, inner life of pictorial, imaginative vision, human beings could perceive the spiritual foundations of the world of the senses. And what their instinctive imagination thus gleaned from the universe they made substantial by using earthly matter and so evolving architecture, sculpture, painting, music and other arts. They gave shape to the fruits of their knowledge in outer material forms. With their human faculties, human beings copied divine creation, giving visible form to all that had first flowed into them as science and knowledge. In short, their art mirrored before their senses all that their forces of knowledge had first assimilated. In weakened form we find this faculty once again in Goethe, when out of his own knowledge and artistic conviction he spoke these significant words: 'Beauty is a manifestation of the secret laws of nature, without which they would remain for ever hidden from us.' And again: 'He before whom nature begins to unveil her open secrets is conscious of an irresistible yearning for art, nature's worthiest expression.'

Such a conception shows that human beings are fundamentally predisposed to view both science and art as two aspects of one and the same truth. This they could do in primeval ages, when knowledge brought them inner satisfaction as it arose in the forms of ideas before their souls, and when the beauty that enchanted them could be made visible to their senses in the arts—for experiences such as these were the essence of earlier civilizations.

What is our position today? As a result of everything that intellectual abstraction has brought in its train, we build up scientific systems of knowledge from which, as far as possible, art is eliminated. It is felt to be positively sinful to introduce art in any way into science, and anyone who is found guilty of this in a scientific book is at once condemned as a dilettante. Our knowledge must be sober, it must be objective, it is said. Art may only supply what has nothing to do with objectivity, but only arises from the arbitrary will of man. A deep abyss thus opens between knowledge and art, and the human being no longer finds any means of crossing it. But it is to his own undoing that he no longer finds a means of crossing it. When he applies the science that is valued because of its freedom from art, he is led indeed to a marvellous knowledge of nature — but of nature devoid of life. The wonderful achievements of science are fully acknowledged by us, yet science is dumb before the mystery of the human being. Look where you will in science today and you will find wonderful answers to the problems of outer nature, but no answers to the riddle of the human being. He is not accessible to the laws of science. Why is this? Heretical as it sounds to modern ears, this is the reason: the moment we draw near to the human being with the laws of nature, we must pass over into the realm of art. A heresy indeed, for people will certainly say: 'That is no longer science. If you try to understand the human being with the artistic sense you are not following the laws of observation and strict logic to which you must always adhere.' However emphatically it may be held that this approach to the human being is unscientific because it is artistic, the human being is nonetheless an artistic creation of nature. All kinds of arguments may be advanced to the effect that this way of artistic understanding is thoroughly unscientific, but the fact remains that human beings cannot be grasped by purely scientific modes of cognition. And so — in spite of all our science — we come to a halt before the human being.

Only if we are sufficiently unbiased can we realize that we must turn to something else, that scientific intellectuality must here be allowed to pass over into the domain of art. Science itself must become art if we would approach the secrets of a person's being.

Now if we follow this path with all our inner forces of soul, not only observing in an outwardly artistic sense, but taking the appropriate path of development, we can allow scientific intellectuality to flow over into what I have described as imagination in my book *How to Know Higher Worlds*. This 'imaginative knowledge' — today an object of such suspicion and opposition — is indeed possible when the kind of thinking that otherwise gives itself up passively to the outer world, a thinking more and more prevalent today, is roused to a living and positive activity. The difficulty of speaking of these things today is not that one is speaking in contradiction of the scientific habits of our age, but that at bottom one is speaking against the whole of modern civilization. There is an increasing tendency today to disregard activity in thinking — inward, active participation in it — and to surrender oneself to the sequence of events, letting thinking just run on in its train, without doing anything oneself.

This state of affairs began with the demand for the material illustration of spiritual things. Take the case of a lecture on spiritual subjects. Visible evidence is out of the question, because words are the only available media — one cannot summon the invisible by some magical process. All that can be done is to stimulate thought and assume that the audience will inwardly energize their thinking into following what can only be indicated by the words. Yet nowadays it will frequently happen that many of the listeners—I do not, of course, refer to those who are sitting in this hall—begin to yawn, because they imagine that thinking ought to be passive, and then they fall asleep because they are not following the subject actively. People like everything to be demonstrated to the eye, illustrated by means of lantern-slides or the like, so that it is unnecessary to think at all. Indeed, they cannot think. That was the beginning, and it has gone still further. In a performance of *Hamlet*, for instance, one must be involved in the action as well as the spoken word in order to understand it. But today the drama has been deserted for the cinema where one does not need to make any effort at all; the pictures roll off the projector and can be watched quite inertly. And so the human being's own inner activity of thought has gradually been lost. But it is this which must be grasped. Then we will perceive that thinking is not simply something which can be stimulated from outside, but represents an inward force within a person's being.

The kind of thinking current in our modern civilization is only one aspect of the force of thought. If we observe it inwardly, from the other side as it were, it is revealed as the force that builds up the human being from childhood. Before this can be understood, the inner, sculptured force that transforms abstract thought into pictures must come into play. Then, after the necessary efforts have been made, we reach the stage I have called in my book the beginning of meditation. At this point we not only begin to transform ability into art, but thought is raised into Imagination. We stand in a world of Imagination, knowing that it is not a creation of our own fantasy but an actual, objective world. We are fully conscious that although we do not as yet possess this objective world itself in the imaginative picture, we have the pictorial quality of it. And the next point to realize is that we must get beyond the picture.

It requires hard work to achieve such inner creative thinking — thinking that does not merely contain pictures of fantasy but pictures bearing their own reality within them. Next, however, we must be able to eliminate the whole of this creative activity again; we must accomplish a first inwardly moral act. For it does indeed constitute a moral action in the inner being of a person if we have taken all the trouble to achieve this pictorial-active thinking (and you can read in my book how much effort this requires), if we apply all the forces of the soul and exert the powers of the self to their very utmost, in order then, after this utmost exertion, to eliminate once more what has been gained in this way. A person must have developed the highest fruits of this thinking in his own being, raised to the level of meditation, and he must then be capable of selflessness. He must be able to eliminate all that has been thus acquired. This is different from not having anything, not having won anything in the first place. And now if he has first of all made every effort to strengthen the self in this way, and then destroys the results of this once more through his own powers so that his consciousness becomes empty, the spiritual world surges into his consciousness; the spiritual world enters his being. Then we can see that spiritual forces of cognition are required for knowledge of the spiritual world. We described active picture-thinking as Imagination. When the spiritual world pours into the consciousness that has, in turn, been emptied by the greatest conceivable effort, it does so by way of what can be called Inspiration. Having gone through Imagination, we can make ourselves worthy through the moral act described above to grasp the spiritual world lying behind external nature and the human being.

I will now attempt to show you how from this point we are led over to religion.

Let me draw your attention to the following. To the extent that anthroposophy strives for true Imagination, it leads not only to knowledge or to art that in itself is of the nature of a picture, but to the spiritual reality contained in the picture. Anthroposophy bridges the gulf between knowledge and art in such a way that at a higher level, suited to modern life and the present age, the unity of science and art which humanity has abandoned can enter civilization once again. This unity must be reattained, for the schism between science and art has disrupted the very being of man. To pass from the state of disruption to unity and inner harmony—it is for this above all that the modern human being must strive.

Thus far I have spoken of the harmony between science

and art. In the third part of the lecture I will develop the subject further in connection with religion and morality.

Knowledge that thus draws the creative activity of the universe into itself can flow directly into art, and this same path from knowledge to art can be extended and continued. It was continued in this way through the powers of the old imaginative knowledge which also found the way, without any intervening gap, into the life of religion. A person who applied himself to this kind of knowledge — primitive and instinctive though it was in early humanity — did not experience it as something external, for in his knowing and thinking he felt that the divinity of the world lived in him, that the creativity of the divine passed over into the artistic creativeness of the human being. Then the way could be found to raise what the human being impressed on matter through art to still higher sanctification. The activity which he made his own as he embodied the divine-spiritual in outer material substance could then be extended into acts in which he was fully conscious that he, as a human being, was expressing the will of the divine powers of the world. He felt himself pervaded by divine creative power, and as the path was followed from the elaboration of material substance to human action, art passed over, by way of ritual, into the service of the divine. Artistic creation became service to God. What is done in the religious ritual represents the consecrated artistic deeds of ancient humanity. Artistic deed was raised into religious deed, the glorification of God through matter into devotion to God through the service of religious ritual. And as human beings thus bridged the gulf between art and religion, there arose a religion in full harmony with knowledge and with art. It may have been primitive and instinctive, but this knowledge was none the less a true picture and as such it could lead human deeds to become, in the acts of ritual, a direct portrayal of the divine.

In this way the transition from art to religion was made possible. Is it still possible with our present-day mode of knowledge? Ancient clairvoyant perception revealed to the human being pictorially the spiritual element in every creature and process of nature, and through the surrender and devotion of the human being to the spirit within the processes of nature the all-pervading, all-creative spirituality of the cosmos passed over into religious ritual.

How do we know the world today? Once again, to describe is better than criticism, for as the following lectures will show, the development of our present mode of knowledge was a necessity in the history of humankind. Today I am merely presenting you with a number of thoughts. We have gradually lost our once spiritual insight into the being and processes of nature. We take pride in eliminating the spirit in our observation of nature, finally reaching such hypothetical conceptions as attribute the origin of our planet to the movements of a primeval nebula. Mechanical events in this nebula are said to be the origin of all the kingdoms of nature, even including the human being. And according to these same laws, which loom so large in our whole would-be objective mode of thinking, this earth must finally end through so-called heat death. All ideals achieved by human beings, having proceeded as a kind of mirage of nature, will disappear until at the end there will remain only the tomb of earthly existence.

If this line of thought is recognized as true by science, and people are honest and brave enough to face its inevitable consequences, they cannot but admit that all religious and moral life is also a mirage and must remain so! Yet the human being cannot endure this thought, and so must cling to the remnants of ancient times, when religion and morality had achieved harmony with knowledge and with art. Religion and morality today do not spring creatively out of a person's inner being; they rest on tradition and are a heritage from ages when all things revealed themselves through the instinctive life of human beings, when God — and the moral world with him — were both made manifest. Our strivings for knowledge today are able to reveal neither God nor a moral world. Science does not see beyond the animal species — the human being is cast out. Honest thinking can find no bridge over the gulf between knowledge and the religious life.

All true religions have sprung from Inspiration. True, the early form of Inspiration was not so conscious as that which is now required, yet it was there instinctively and the religions rightly trace their origin back to it. Such faiths as no longer recognize living Inspiration and revelation from the spirit in the immediate present will have to be content with tradition. But such faiths lack any inner vitality, any direct motivating power of religious life. This motivating power and vitality must be regained, for only by this means can our social organism be healed.

To be able to make God present in the world—this is true morality. Nature cannot lead the human being to morality. Only that which lifts him above nature, filling him with the divine-spiritual—this alone can lead the human being to morality. Only the Intuition which affects the human being when through the religious life he places himself in the spirit can fill him with real, inmost morality, at once human and divine. The attainment of Inspiration thus rebuilds the bridge which once existed instinctively in human civilization between religion and morality. As knowledge leads upwards through art to the heights of supersensory life, so spiritual heights are brought down to earthly existence through religious worship, so that we can fill this existence with the impulse of an essential, primal, direct morality actually experienced by the human being. Thus the human being himself in truth becomes the individual bearer of a life imbued by morality and filled with an immediate moral impulse. Morality will then be a creation of the individual himself and the last abyss between religion and morality will be bridged. The intuition which permeated primitive man as he enacted his ritual will be recreated in a new form, and a morality truly corresponding with modern conditions will arise from a modern religious life. We need this for the renewal of our civilization. We need it in order that what today is mere heritage, mere tradition, may spring again into original life. This primordial impulse is required by the complications of modern society, which are threatening to spread chaos through the world. We need harmony between knowledge, art, religion and morality. In a new form, we need to pursue this path that leads away from the earth and along which we acquire our knowledge by passing through Inspiration and through the arts to the direct life in the supersensory sphere, to a grasp of the supersensory element, so that we can again bring it back down into social life on earth, having experienced it in religion and transformed it into will. We can grapple with the social question to its full extent only when we see it as one of morality and religion, and this we cannot do until our moral and religious life is based on spiritual knowledge. Once human beings achieve spiritual knowledge again, they will be able to do what is needed to link their further evolution with its instinctive origins. They will find what must be found to heal humanity—harmony between science, art, religion and morality.

8. The Spiritual Ground of Education

In Oxford, Steiner talked about questions of morality and childhood and how this could be developed for later life. His words are inspirational for the teacher or carer and full of respect for the child itself. Over the last few years these have become current social problems, with some children seemingly having lost their way and being involved in acts that society finds abhorrent. As traditional values lose their force, new values have to be found whereby we can tolerate, understand and have respect for each other. This is not a question of knowledge and, indeed, it has increasingly been shown that burdening children with knowledge they cannot digest or deal with actually increases their difficulties. That a growing number of children have psychiatric disorders, and drugs like Ritalin are more readily prescribed to control behaviour, is a symptom of a malaise that cannot be ignored and impinges on school responsibilities. Approaching education as a removal of hindrances is a positive attitude to this, and one that can be embarked on with optimism and trust in the real underlying positive qualities that every child has. The science of genetics has shown there is no such thing as an evil gene. But there are propensities and a school based on this insight is where we can nurture what is positive and humane without becoming deterministic or coercive.

If we now turn to the moral aspect, the question is how we can best get the child to develop moral impulses. And here we are dealing with the most important of all educational questions. Now we do not endow a child with moral impulses by giving him commands, by saying you must do this, this has to be done, this is good, by wanting to prove that a thing is good and must be done. Neither do we do so by saying this is bad, this is wicked, you must not do this, and by wanting to prove that a certain thing is bad. A child does not as yet have the intellectual attitude of an adult towards good and evil, towards the whole world of morality — it has to grow up to it. And this it will only do on reaching puberty, when the rhythmical system has accomplished its essential task and the intellectual powers are ripe for complete development. Then the human being may experience the satisfaction of forming moral judgements in the context of life itself. We must not graft moral judgements onto the child. We must lay the foundation for moral judgement in such a way that when the child awakens at puberty it can form its own moral judgements from observation of life.

The way not to attain this is to give finite commands to a child. We can achieve it, however, if we work by examples or by presenting pictures to the child's imagination, for instance through biographies or descriptions of good people or bad people, or by inventing circumstances which present a picture, an imagination of goodness to the child's mind. For since the rhythmical system is particularly active in the child during this period, it can feel pleasure and displeasure—not judgement as to good and evil but sympathy with the good which the child sees presented in an image or antipathy to the evil which he thus experiences. It is not a case of appealing to the child's intellect, of saying 'Thou shalt' or 'Thou shalt not', but of fostering aesthetic judgement so that the child can begin to take pleasure in goodness, can feel sympathy when it sees goodness, and feel dislike and antipathy when it sees evil. This is a very different thing from working on the intellect, by way of precepts formulated by the intellect. For the child will only be awake to such precepts when it is no longer our business to educate the child, namely, when it is an adult and learns from life itself. And we should not rob the child of the satisfaction of awakening to morality of its own accord. The way to avoid doing so is to give it the right preparation during the rhythmical period of its life, if we train it to take an aesthetic pleasure in goodness, an aesthetic dislike of evil—that is, if here, too, we work through imagery.

Otherwise, when the child awakens after puberty it will feel an inward restriction. It will not perhaps realize this restriction consciously but throughout its subsequent life it will lack the important experience that morality has awakened within it, moral judgement has developed. We cannot achieve this inner satisfaction by means of abstract moral instruction; it must be properly prepared by working in this manner with the child's morality.

Thus it is a case of 'how' a thing is done. And we can see this both in that part of life which is concerned with the external world and that part of life concerned with morality, when we study the realm of nature in the best way and when we know how morals can best be developed in the rhythmical system—in the system of breathing and blood circulation. If we know how to introduce the spirit into the physical and if we can come to observe how the spirit continuously permeates the physical we shall be able to educate in the right way.

While a knowledge of the human being is required in the first instance for the art of education and teaching, in practice the effect of such a spiritual outlook on the teacher's state of mind is of the greatest importance. And what this is can best be shown in relation to the attitude of many of our contemporaries.

Every age without doubt has its shadow side and there is much in past ages we have no wish to revive. Nevertheless, anyone who can observe the historical life of human beings with a certain intuitive sense will perceive that in this our own age many people have very little inner joy; on the contrary, they are beset by heavy doubts and questions as to the future. This age has less capacity than any other for deriving answers to its problems from the universe, the world at large. Though I may be very unhappy in myself, and with good reason, yet there is always a possibility of finding something in the universe that can counterbalance my unhappiness. But modern people do not have the strength to find consolation in a view of the universe when their personal circumstances makes them downcast. Why is this? Because in their education and development modern people have little opportunity to acquire a feeling of gratitude—gratitude, namely, that we should be alive at all as human beings within this universe. Properly speaking, all our feelings should be based on a fundamental feeling of gratitude that the cosmic world has given us birth and given us a place within itself. A philosophy that concludes with abstract observations and does not flow out in gratitude towards the universe is not a complete philosophy. The final chapter of every philosophy, in its effect on human feeling at all events, should be gratitude towards the cosmic powers. This feeling is essential in a teacher and educator, and it should be instinctive in every person who has the nurture of a child entrusted to her or him. Therefore the first thing of importance that needs to be acquired in spiritual knowledge is the thankfulness that a child has been given into our keeping by the universe.

In this respect, reverence for the child, reverence and thankfulness, cannot be divided. There is only one attitude towards a child that can give us the right impulse in education and nurture and that is a religious attitude, neither more nor less. We feel religious with regard to many things. A flower in a meadow can make us feel religious if we take it as the product of the divine-spiritual order of the world. We feel religious in the face of lightning flashes in the clouds if we see them in relation to the divine-spiritual order of the world. And above all, we must feel religious towards the child, for it comes to us from the heart of the universe as the highest manifestation of the nature of the universe, a bringer of tidings as to what the world is. This mood contains one of the most important impulses for educational method. Educational method is of a different nature from the method devoted to non-spiritual things. Educational method essentially involves a religious and moral impulse in the teacher or educator.

Now some may say that although people today are so terribly objective with regard to many things — things possibly of less vital importance — yet there will be some who will think it a great tragedy that they should have a religious feeling for a child who may turn out to be a good-for-nothing. But why must I regard it as a tragedy to have a child who turns out to be a good-for-nothing? Today, as we said before, there are many parents even in this terribly objective age who will admit that their children are good-for-nothings whereas this was not the case in former times; then every child was good in its parents' eyes. At all events, this was a better attitude than the modern one. Nevertheless, we do get a feeling of tragedy if we receive a difficult child as a gift from spiritual worlds and as a manifestation of the highest. But we must live through this feeling of tragedy. For this very feeling of tragedy will help us over the rocks and crags of education. If we can feel thankfulness even for a naughty child, and feel the tragedy of it, and can rouse ourselves to overcome this feeling of tragedy, we shall then be in a position to feel a proper gratitude to the divine world; for we must learn to perceive how what is bad can also be a divine thing, though this is a very complicated matter. Gratitude must permeate teachers and educators of children throughout the period up to the change of teeth; it must be their fundamental mood.

Then we come to that period of a child's development which is based principally on the rhythmic system, in which, as we have seen, we must work artistically in education. This we shall never achieve unless we can combine the religious attitude we have towards the child with a love of our educational activity; we must saturate our educational practice with love. Between the change of teeth and puberty nothing that is not born of love for the educational deed itself has any effect on the child. We must tell ourselves with regard to the child that, however clever a teacher or educator may be, the child reveals to us in his life infinitely significant spiritual and divine things. But we, on our part, must surround with love the spiritual deed we do for the child in education. Hence there must be no pedagogy and didactics of a purely intellectual kind, but only such guidance as can help the teacher to carry out his education with loving enthusiasm.

In the Waldorf school, the character of a teacher is far more important than any technical ability he or she may have acquired in an intellectual way. The important thing is that the teacher should not only be able to love the child but to love the method he uses, to love the whole process. Only to love the children is not enough for a teacher. To love teaching, to love educating and love it with objectivity — this constitutes the spiritual foundation of spiritual, moral and physical education. And if we can acquire such a proper love for education, for teaching, we will be able to ensure the proper development of the child up to the age of puberty so that when that period arrives we can truly hand him over to freedom, to the free use of his own intelligence.

If we have received the child in religious reverence, if we have educated him in love up to the time of puberty, then our proper course after this will be to leave the young person's spirit free, and to base our interaction with him or her on terms of equality. Our aim is to let the spirit be awakened. When the child reaches puberty we shall best achieve our aim of giving the child over to the free use of his intellectual and spiritual powers if we respect the spirit and say to ourselves: you can remove hindrances from the spirit, physical hindrances and also, up to a point, hindrances of the soul. What the spirit has to learn it learns because you have removed the impediments. If we remove impediments, the spirit will develop in contact with life itself even in very early youth. Our rightful place as educators is to be removers of hindrances.

Hence we must see to it that we do not make the children into copies of ourselves, that we do not seek forcibly and tyrannically to perpetuate what was in ourselves in those who, in the natural course of things, develop beyond us. Each child in every age brings something new into the world from divine regions, and it is our task as educators to remove obstacles of the body and soul out of its way, to remove hindrances so that its spirit may enter into life in full freedom. These then must be regarded as the three golden rules of the art of education, rules which must permeate the teacher's whole attitude and all the impulses underlying his or her work. The golden rules that must be embraced by the teacher's whole being, not just as theory are: reverent gratitude to the world in the person of the child which we contemplate every day, for the child presents a task set us by divine worlds, leading to thankfulness to the universe; love for our tasks with regard to the child; and respect for the freedom of the child — a freedom we must not put at risk, for we educate the child to such freedom that it may stand in freedom in the world at our side.

9. The Role of Caring in Education

Through gratitude and love human beings learn to care for both the world in which they live and their fellow beings that inhabit it. Steiner reiterates throughout his lectures the importance of loving devotion towards what one is doing and an understanding interest in what others are doing. These moral values stand at the core of the Waldorf curriculum and pedagogical methods and transcend any cultural, ethnic, religious and/or class differences that we, as educators, or the children may have. In a Waldorf school the children are helped in developing these values in a developmentally appropriate way not only by words but also by the character and bearing of the teacher.

There is rather a telling anecdote concerning Rudolf Steiner's visit to England in August 1924. One afternoon he made an announcement to his audience that, before continuing the teachers' course he was giving, he had an important statement to make. He then began to unwrap the paper from around a piece of chalk as if he intended to illustrate his words on the blackboard, and then held the paper that was to be discarded in his hands looking for a waste-paper basket. However, there was none in his proximity. At this point one of the participants called out: 'Please, Herr Doctor, just let the waste paper drop into the corner and we will tidy it up later.' Steiner, however, waited until a basket was made available and very deliberately dropped the pieces of paper into it. He then said, 'What I intended to say was this. You may have an enormous amount of pedagogical knowledge, but when you drop the wrapping from a piece of chalk on the floor and do not place it into a waste-paper basket then all your knowledge is of no value.'[14]

Care is about being awake to the moment and at the same time being aware of the consequences of any action or inaction. We could also call it moral ecology. Care is part of our spiritual nature and its ethical dimension can make us better teachers. From the seemingly mundane care of the teaching space to care for the institution we work in, from care for the individual child to care for the subject as a manifestation of the immense possibilities of human knowledge, we can awaken a sense of caring in ourselves and that is, in turn, the quality of what we do and set out to achieve. The quality is the care. It can manifest itself in direct action as well as in discussion and papers.

Consideration of the relationship of the growing child to its surroundings raises questions of ethical and social education. It is these two issues we will consider today, even if only briefly and sketchily because of shortness of time. Once again, the crux of the matter is knowing how to adapt oneself to the individuality of the growing child. At the same time, you will have to bear in mind that as a teacher and educator you are part of the social setting and that you personally bring the social environment and its ethical attitudes to the growing pupil. Again, pedagogical principles and methods must be formulated in such a way that they offer every chance of reaching the true nature of the child which we have to learn to know in accordance with what has been briefly shown here in the last few days. As always, a great deal depends on how one brings one's content to the pupils in their various ages and stages.

Now there are three human virtues we need to consider here, on the one hand with regard to the child's own development, and on the other seen against the background of society in general. They are the three fundamental virtues. Firstly, all that lives in willing gratitude; secondly, all that lives in the will to love; and thirdly, all that lives in the will to do one's duty. Fundamentally, these are the three principal human virtues, to a certain extent encompassing all other virtues.

Generally speaking, people are far too little aware of what, in this context, I should like to call gratitude or thankfulness. And yet gratitude is a virtue which, if it is to play its proper part in the human soul, has to grow up with the child. It is something that has to flow into the human being already at the time when the growth forces, working in the child in an inward direction, are at their liveliest, and when they are at the peak of their shaping and moulding activities. Gratitude is something that has to be developed out of the bodily-religious relationship which I have described as being the dominant feature in the child from birth till the loss of the milk teeth. Yet at the same time it is also something that will develop quite spontaneously during this first period of life, provided the child is treated rightly. All that is flowing from its inner being with devotion and love towards what is coming from the periphery through the parents or other educators, and all that finds outer expression in the child's imitation, will be imbued with a natural mood of gratitude. We only have to behave in ways worthy of the child's gratitude for it to flow towards us, especially so in the first period of life. And then this gratitude develops further by streaming into the forces of growth which make the limbs grow and which even alter the chemical composition of the blood and other body liquids. This gratitude lives in the physical body and it must dwell in it, since otherwise it would not be anchored deeply enough.

Now it would be quite wrong to constantly remind the child that it must be thankful for everything that comes from its surroundings. On the contrary, an atmosphere of gratitude should grow naturally, simply through the children's witnessing the gratitude felt by their elders as they receive what is freely given to them by their fellow human beings, and also in the way they express their gratitude. In this situation one would also cultivate the habit of feeling grateful by letting the child imitate what is done in its surroundings. If a child will say 'thank you' quite naturally—not in response to exhortations but simply out of imitation—it does something that will be of great benefit for the whole of its life. For out of this there will develop an all-embracing gratitude towards the whole world.

It is the cultivation of this universal gratitude towards the world that is of paramount importance. It need not always be in one's consciousness, it may simply live in the background of one's feeling life, so that someone, at the end of a strenuous day, can experience thankfulness upon entering a beautiful meadow full of flowers—to give an example. Such a subconscious feeling of gratitude may rise up in us every time we look at nature. It may be felt every morning when the sun rises. It may emerge when beholding any of nature's phenomena. And if we only conduct ourselves rightly in front of the children, a correspondingly graduated feeling of thankfulness will develop in them for all that comes to them from the people living around them, from the way they speak, smile or deal with them.

This universal mood of gratitude is the basis of a truly religious attitude. For it is not always recognized that this universal sense of gratitude, provided it grips the whole human being during the first period of life, will engender yet something else. For in human life love will flow into everything, if only the right conditions offer themselves for its development. The possibility of a more intensive experience of love, reaching the physical level, is given only during the second period of life between the change of teeth and puberty. But that first tender love, so deeply embodied in the inner being of the child, without as yet working in an outward direction—this tender blossom will take firm roots through the development of gratitude. And love, born out of the experience of gratitude during the first period of the child's life, this is the love of God. One ought to realize that just as one has to dig the roots of a plant into the soil in order, later on, to receive its blossom, so one has to plant gratitude into the soul of the child because it is the root of the love of God. The love of God will develop out of universal gratitude, as the blossom develops out of the root.

We should pay attention to these things because in the abstract we usually know quite well how they ought to be. Yet, in actual life situations, all too often they turn out to be quite different. In theory it is easy enough to state that people ought to carry the love of God within themselves, and this is as right as can be. But such demands made in the abstract have a peculiar habit of never seeing the light of day in practice.

I would like to return to what I said during one of the last few days. It is easy enough to think of the function of a stove in the following way: 'You are a stove and we have to put you here because we want to heat the room. Your categorical imperative—the true categorical "stove imperative"—tells you that you are obliged to heat the room.' We know only too well that this in itself will not make the slightest difference in the temperature of the room. But we can also save our sermonizing and, instead, simply light the stove and heat it with suitable logs. Then it will radiate its warmth without being reminded of its categorical imperative. And this is how it is when during the various stages of childhood we bring to the child the right thing at the right time. If, during its first period of life, we create an atmosphere of gratitude around the child, and if we carry out something else, of which I shall speak later, then, out of this gratitude towards the world, towards the entire universe, and also out of an inner thankfulness for being in this world at all (which is something that should ensoul all people), there will grow the most deep-seated and warmest piety — not the kind that dwells on one's lips or in one's thoughts only, but a piety that will pervade the entire human being and that will be upright, honest and true. As for gratitude, it has to grow. But this can happen with the intensity necessary for such a soul and spiritual quality only if it develops from the child's tender life-stirrings during the time from birth to its change of teeth. And then this gratitude will become the root of the love of God. It is the foundation of the love of God.

Knowing all this will make us realize that when we receive children into class one, we must also take into consideration what kind of lives they have led prior to reaching school age. There really ought to be a direct contact with the parental home, that is, with what has gone on before the child entered school. This contact should always be striven for, because the teachers ought to have a fairly clear picture of how the child's present situation was influenced by the social conditions and the milieu in which it grew up. Then, at school, they will find plenty of opportunities of rectifying any possible obstacles. But for this to happen, knowledge of the child's home background, through contact with the parents, is of course absolutely essential. It is necessary for teachers to be able to observe how certain characteristics have developed in a child simply by watching and imitating mother at home. To be aware of this is very important when the child begins its schooling. It is just as much part of teaching as what is done in the classroom.

These matters must not be overlooked if one wants to build up an effective and properly founded education. We have already seen that during the years between the child's change of teeth and the coming of puberty the development of a sense for the authority of the teacher is both natural and essential. Out of it there then grows the second fundamental virtue, which is love. At that time of life the child is in the process of also developing the physical basis of love. But one has to see love in its true light. For, owing to the prevailing materialistic attitudes of our time, the concept of love has become very one-sided and narrow. And since a materialistic outlook tends to see love only in terms of sexual love, it generally traces all manifestations of love back to a hidden sexuality. In an instance of what I called 'dilettantism squared' the day before yesterday, we find, if not in every case, that at least many psychologists trace human traits back to sexual origins, even if they have nothing to do with sex whatsoever. To balance such an attitude, the teacher must have acquired at least some measure of appreciation for the universal nature of love. For it is not only sexual love that begins to develop between the child's second dentition and puberty, but love in its fullest sense, love for everything in the world. Sexual love is only one aspect of love that develops at this time of life. At that age one can witness how love of nature and also love of one's fellow human beings awakens in the child, and the teacher needs to have a strong conception of how sexual love represents only one facet, one single chapter in life's book of love. If one realizes this, one will also know how to assign to sexual love its proper place in life. Today, for many people who look at life with theoretical eyes, sexual love has become a kind of Moloch devouring his own offspring in that — if their views were true — sexual love would devour all other forms of love.

Love develops in the human soul in a way different from that of gratitude. Gratitude has to grow with the growing human being and this is the reason why it has to be planted at the time when the child's growth forces are at their strongest. Love, on the other hand, has to awaken. The development of love actually does resemble the process of waking and, like it, it has to remain more in the region of the soul. The gradual coming into being of love is a slow awakening, until the final stage of this process has been reached. Observe for a moment what happens when one wakes up in the morning. At first there is a dim awareness of vague notions, perhaps first sensations begin to stir, slowly the eyelids wrest themselves free from the closed position, gradually the outer world comes to the aid of one's awakening, and finally the moment of waking passes over into the physical body.

This is also how it is with the awakening of love — except that in the child this process takes some seven years. At first love begins to stir when sympathy is aroused for all that is being taught during the early days at school. If we begin to approach the child with the kind of imagery I have described, we can see how love especially comes to meet this activity. Everything has to be saturated with this love. At that stage, love has a profoundly soul-like and tender quality. If one compares it with the daily process of waking up, one would still be deeply asleep, or at least in a state of sleeping dreaming. (Here I am referring to the child's condition of course—the teacher must not be in a dream, although this seems to happen all too frequently!) This condition then yields to a stronger jolt into wakefulness. And in what I described yesterday and the day before regarding the ninth and tenth year, and especially in the time leading up to the twelfth year, love of nature awakens in the child. Only then do we see it truly emerging.

Before this stage, the child's relationship to nature is totally different. At that time it still has a great love for all that belongs to the fairy world of nature, a love that has to be nourished by a creative and pictorial approach. Love for the realities in nature awakens only afterwards. And at this point we are faced with a particularly difficult task. Into all that belongs to the curriculum at this time of life, causality, the study of lifeless matter, an understanding of historical interconnections, the beginnings of physics and chemistry, into all this the teacher has to introduce—and here I am not joking, but speaking in deep earnest—the teacher has to introduce an element of grace. In geometry or physics lessons, for example, there is every need for the teacher to allow real grace to enter into the teaching. All lessons should be pervaded with an air of graciousness and above all, the subjects must never be allowed to become sour. So often, just during the ages from $11\frac{1}{2}$, or $11\frac{3}{4}$ to 14 or 15, work in these subjects suffers so much by becoming unpalatable and sour. What the pupils have to learn about the refraction and reflection of light or about the measurement of surface areas in a dome is so often spoken of not with grace, but with an air of sourness.

Just at this time of life the teacher has to be mindful of the need for a certain 'soul breathing' in the lessons, which communicates itself to the pupils in a very strange way — 'soul-breathing' must be possible. Ordinary breathing consists of inhaling and exhaling. In most cases, or at least on many occasions, teachers in their physics and geometry lessons only breathe out with their souls. They do not breathe in — and it is the outgoing breath that produces this acidity. I am referring to the kind of out-breathing of soul that expresses itself in dull and monotonous descriptions, infusing all content with an added seriousness of inflated proportions. Seriousness does have its place, but not in an exaggerated form.

On the other hand, an inbreathing of soul brings with it an inherent sense of humour that is always ready to sparkle, both inside and outside the classroom or whenever there is an opportunity for teachers and pupils to be together. The only possible hindrance to such radiating humour could be the teachers themselves. The children certainly would not stand in its way, neither would the various subjects, provided they were handled with the right touch during this particular age. If teachers could feel so at home in their subjects that they were entirely free from having to chew over their content while giving lessons, then they might find themselves in a position where even reflected light was liable to crack a joke or where the dome might calculate its surface area with a winning smile. Of course, jokes should not be planned beforehand, nor should they be forced upon the classroom situation. Everything should be tinged with spontaneous humour, which is inherent in the content and not artificially grafted onto it. This is the crux of the matter. Humour has to be found in the things themselves and, above all, it should not even be necessary to look for it. At best, teachers who have prepared their lessons properly need to bring a certain order and discipline into the ideas that will come to them while teaching—for this is what happens if one is well prepared. But the opposite is equally possible; if one has not prepared the lessons adequately, one will feel deprived of ideas because one still has to wrestle with the lesson content. This spoils a healthy out-breathing of the soul and shuts out the humour-filled air it needs. These are the important points one has to bear in mind at this particular age.

If teaching thus follows its proper course, the awakening of love will happen in such a way that the pupil's soul and spirit are rightly integrated into the human organization when the final stage of this awakening, namely, the approach of puberty, begins. For this is the time when what first developed in the child's soul in such a tender and subsequently in a more robust way is finally able to grip the bodily nature in the right and proper manner.

Now you may be wondering what teachers have to do in order to be capable of carrying out their tasks in the way described. And here we have to consider something I would like to call the social aspect of the teaching profession, the importance of which is far too little recognized. Too often we come across an image a certain age has associated with the teaching profession, whose members are not generally respected and honoured as they should be. (This is not, however, the case in ancient times.) Only if society looks upon teachers with the due respect for their calling, only if it recognizes that teachers stand in the forefront of bringing new impulses into our civilization—and this not only when speeches are made from a political platform—only then will teachers receive the moral support they need for their work. Such an attitude or, perhaps better still, such a sentiment, would pave the way towards the acquisition of a wider and more comprehensive view of life. For this is what teachers need—they too need be fully integrated into life. They need not only proper qualifications in educational principles and methods, not only a specialist training for their various subjects, but above all they need something that will renew itself ever and again, namely, a conception of life that pulsates livingly through their souls. What they need is a deep understanding of life itself. They need far more than what can pass from their lips as they stand in front of their classes. All this has to flow into the making of a teacher. Strictly speaking, the question of education should be part of the social question, and it needs to embrace not only the actual teaching schools, but also the inner development of the teaching faculty.

10. The Roots of Education and the Kingdom of Childhood

The curriculum of the Steiner school is extraordinarily broad and covers a multitude of subjects. Many are taught over a three or four week period for two hours or so every morning, to enable the child to really inhabit the subject. Out of this the pupils produce their own textbooks and record of work that is also presented artistically and is an achievement to be proud of. This morning lesson is then followed by subject lessons that, like foreign languages or maths, need continuous practice. Steiner gave many indications as to how all these could be taught, especially in lower grades, but yet insisted that it all basically came down to the insights and creativity of the teachers themselves. This of course has fundamental implications for teacher education and the way the schools are run. The teacher meetings, as well as conducting the business of running the school, are expected to have the quality of research and further training. The curriculum he suggests starts with the basic skills of numeracy and literacy that are discussed in these two lectures, and then journeys through geography, the sciences, history, literature, building, farming, astronomy, philosophy and so on, so that it eventually covers as many fields of human activity and knowledge as possible. The ideal outcome is that the students are well prepared for the changing world and have an appreciation and under-standing of its complexities, as well as having retained an enthusiastic willingness to learn and a boundless curiosity. As shown here, everything taught in a school has a sense of values attached, either explicit or implicit, and it is these values that should be explored and made conscious by the teacher.

In aiming at an art of education, we must provide a training which is based on a knowledge of the human being. One hesitates to say these things because they are so difficult to grasp. But it is an error to believe that the ideas that have arisen from natural science can give us an understanding of the human being, and to be aware of this error is one of the vital conditions for the progress of the art of education. It is only when one looks at the child from this point of view that one can see, for example, what radical and far-reaching changes occur with the coming of the second teeth, when the memory becomes a pictorial memory and is no longer attached to the physical body but to the etheric body. For what is it that really brings forth the second teeth? It is the fact that up to this time the etheric is almost completely bound up with the physical body, and when the first teeth come out something is separated from the physical body. If it were not so, we should get new teeth every seven years. (As people's teeth decay so rapidly nowadays this would seem to be quite a good thing, and dentists would have to look for another job!) When the etheric body is separated off, then what formerly worked in the physical body now works in the realm of soul. If you have a perception for these things and can examine a child's mouth without its knowledge, you will see for yourself that it is so. It is always better that a child does not know that it is being observed. This is why experimental psychology so often fails, because the child knows what is being done. You examine the child's second teeth which have been formed by the etheric body into a modelled image of the memory, and the shape of the teeth created by the etheric will be an indication of how the memory of the child will develop. With the exception of slight alterations of position here or there, you cannot materially change the second teeth once they are through, unless you can really go so far as, for example, the dentist Professor Romer has done. He has written a book on dentistry along the lines of a new art of medicine based on anthroposophical principles, where he speaks of certain changes which can be effected even when the second teeth are all through.

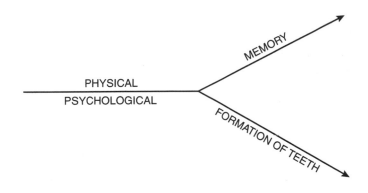

But this need not concern us further. When at the change of teeth the etheric body is loosened and stands alone, then the development of the memory is separated off from the physical element, and remains almost entirely in the element of soul, and this fact can really put the teachers on the right track. For before this change the soul and spirit formed a unity with the physical and etheric elements. After it, the physical, which formerly worked together with the soul, is expressed in the form of the second teeth, and what collaborated with the physical in this process is separated off and is revealed as an increase in the power of forming ideas, and in the formation and reliability of the memory. If you have acquired this insight into human nature you will discover a great deal that will help you in your teaching. You must permeate yourselves with this spiritual knowledge of the human being in a living way, and then your observations of the child will inspire you with ideas and methods for your teaching, and this inner inspiration and enthusiasm will pass over into your practical work. The rules laid down in introductory books on education only produce an abstract activity of the soul, whereas what arises out of an anthroposophical knowledge penetrates into the teacher's will and into his work, and becomes the impulse for all that he does in the classroom.

A living knowledge of the human being brings life and order into the soul of the teacher, but if he only studies methods which arise out of natural science then he may get some clever ideas of what to do with the child but he will not be able to carry them out; for the teacher's skill and practical handling of the child must arise out of the living spirit which is within him, and here purely scientific ideas can find no place. If the teacher can acquire a true knowledge of the human being, then he will notice how when the etheric body is freed at the change of teeth the child has an inner urge to receive everything in the form of pictures; in his own inner being he himself wants to become 'picture'. In the first period of life the impressions do not have this picture-forming tendency but are converted into habit and skill in the child; memory itself is habit and skill. The child wants to imitate everything that it sees going on around him in the movements of his limbs; it has no desire to form any inward pictures. But after the change of teeth you will notice how the child comes to know things quite differently. Now it wants to feel that pictures are arising in his soul, and therefore the teacher must bring everything into a pictorial element in his lessons. This creating of pictures is what the teacher has to understand above everything else.

But when we begin to look at the facts we are immediately confronted with certain contradictions. The child has to learn to read and write, and when it comes to school we take it for granted that he will learn to read first and then to write in connection with its reading. But let us think what the letters really are which we use when we put pen to paper and try to express in writing what is in our mind. What relationship do the printed letters of today have to the original picture-language of olden times? How were we taught these things? We have to teach the children what a capital 'A' and a small 'a' are like, but whatever in the world do these letters have to do with the sound 'A' (as in 'father'). There is no connection at all between the form of the letter A and the sound A. At the time when the art of writing arose, things were different. In certain areas pictorial signs were used and a kind of pictorial painting was employed. True, this became conventionalized later, but to begin with these drawings were copies of the process and feeling of the sounds, so that what one had on the paper was to a certain extent a reproduction of what was living in the soul. But the modern characters are alien to the nature of the little child, and it is small wonder that when certain primitive peoples first saw printed letters they had a peculiar effect on them. When the Europeans came among the native Indians of America and showed them how they expressed their thoughts on paper, the Indians were quite alarmed and thought it was the work of the devil; they were terrified of the little demons who were lurking behind the written letters. They immediately concluded that the Europeans dealt in black magic, for people have a habit of attributing to black magic whatever they cannot understand.

But how does the matter really stand? We know that when we utter the sound 'Ah' we express wonder, admiration. Now it is quite a natural thing to try and reproduce this sound with your whole body and express it in this gesture of your arms. If you copy this gesture (stretching the arms obliquely above the head) then you get the capital A. In your teaching you can for instance begin with such a feeling of wonder, and proceed with the children to a kind of painting-drawing, and thus you can bring their inward and outward experiences into this painting-drawing and drawing-painting.

Now take another example. I tell the child to think of a fish, and I get him to paint it (awkward though this may be). He must do it in a special way, not just anyhow as he might like to, but with the head in front, like this, and the rest of the fish here. The child paints the fish, and thus, by a kind of painting-drawing, drawing-painting, he has

produced a written character. You then tell him to pronounce the word 'fish' — f-i-sh. Now take away the 'i-sh', and from 'fish' you have passed over to his first written letter, 'f'. In this way the child will come to understand how pictorial writing arose, and how it developed into the writing of the present day. The forms were copied and the pictures were abandoned. This is how the drawing of the different sounds arose. You do not need to make a special study of how these things evolved. It is not absolutely necessary for a teacher, for he can develop them out of his own intuition and power of imagination.

Or take the mouth as another example. Let the child paint the upper lip, and then pronounce the word 'mouth'. Leave out the 'outh', and you get the 'M'. In this

way you can relate all the written characters to some reality, and the child will constantly be developing a living, inward activity. So you should teach the children writing first, and let the abstract letters of our present-day writing arise out of concrete reality; if a child learns to write in this way his whole being is engaged in the process. Whereas if you start with reading, then only the head takes part in an abstract way. In writing, the hand must participate too and the whole human being is roused into activity. Thus if you begin with writing, a writing which is developed out of such shaping in pictures, drawing in forms, then in your teaching you will approach the whole being of the child. After this you can proceed to the teaching of reading, and what the child has developed out of his whole being in this painting-drawing can then be understood by the head. This method of teaching writing and reading will of course take longer, but it will have a far greater health-giving effect on the whole earthly life from birth to death.

These things can be done when the practical work of the

school flows out of a real spiritual knowledge of the human being. Such a knowledge can out of its own inner force become the teaching method in our schools. It is this which lives in the desires of those who are seriously seeking for a new art of education, but it can only be found in its true inner being if we are not afraid to seek for full knowledge of the human being, body, soul and spirit.

It is essential that you have some understanding of the real essence of every subject that you teach, so that you do not use things in your teaching that are remote from life itself. Everything that is intimately connected with life can be understood. I could even say that whatever one really understands has this intimate connection with life. This is not the case with abstractions.

Today we find that teachers' ideas are largely abstractions, so that in many respects the teachers themselves are remote from life. This is a source of great difficulties in education and teaching. Just consider the following: imagine that you want to think over how you first came to count things and what really happens when you count. You will probably find that the thread of your recollections breaks somewhere, and that you did once learn to count, but actually you do not really know what you do when you count.

Now all kinds of theories are thought up to teach numbers and counting, and it is customary to act upon such theories. But even when external results can be obtained, the whole being of the child fails to be touched with this kind of counting or with similar things that have no connection with real life. The modern age has proved that it lives in abstractions, by inventing such things as the abacus or bead-frame for teaching. In a business office people can use calculating machines as much as they like (that does not concern us at the moment) but teaching how to use this calculating machine, which is exclusively concerned with the activities of the head, prevents you from the very start from dealing with numbers in accordance with the child's nature.

Counting however should be derived from life itself, and here it is supremely important to know from the beginning that you should not ever expect a child to understand every single thing you teach. Children must take a great deal on authority, but they must take it in a natural, practical way.

Perhaps you may find that what I am now going to say will be rather difficult for the child. But that does not matter. It is of great importance that there should be moments in a person's life when in the thirtieth or fortieth year that person can say to himself: now I understand what in my eighth or ninth year, or even earlier, I took on authority. This awakens new life in a person. But if you look at all the object lessons that are introduced into the teaching of today, you may well be in despair over the way things are trivialized, in order, as the saying goes, to bring them closer to the child's understanding.

Now imagine that you have quite a young child in front of you, one who still moves quite clumsily, and you say: 'There you are, standing before me. And here I take a piece of wood and a knife and I cut the wood into pieces. Can I do that to you?' The child will see that I cannot do it. And now I can say: 'Look, if I can cut the piece of wood in two, the wood is not like you, and you are not like the wood, for I cannot cut you in two like that. So there is a difference between you and the wood. The difference lies in the fact that you are a unit, a "one", and the wood is not a "one". You are a unit and I cannot cut you in two, and therefore I call you "one", a unit.'

You can now gradually proceed to show the child a sign for this 'one'. You make a stroke — I — so that you show it is a unit and you make this stroke for it.

Now you can move on from this comparison between the wood and the child and you can say: 'Look, here is your right hand but you have another hand too, your left hand. If you only had this one hand it could certainly move about everywhere as you do, but if your hand were only to follow the movement of your body you could never touch yourself in the way your two hands can touch each other. For when this hand moves and the other hand moves at the same time, then they can take hold of each other, they can come together. That is different from when you simply move alone. When you walk alone you are a unit. But the one hand can touch the other hand. This is no longer a unit, this is a duality, a "two". See, you are one, but you have two hands.' This you then show like this: II.

In this way you can work out a concept of 'one' and 'two' from the child's own form.

Now you call out another child and say: 'When you two

walk towards each other you can also meet and touch each other; there are two of you, but a third can join you. This is impossible with your hands.' Thus you can proceed to the three: III.

In this manner you can derive numbers out of what the human being is itself. You can lead over to numbers from the human being, who is not an abstraction but a living being.

Then you can say: 'Look, you can find the number two in other places on your body.' The children will think finally of their two legs and feet. Now you say: 'You have seen your neighbour's dog, haven't you? Does the dog also only walk on two feet?' Then the children will come to realize that the four strokes IIII are a picture of the neighbour's dog propped up on four legs, and thus will gradually learn to build up numbers out of life.

The teacher's eyes must always be alert and look at everything with understanding. Now you naturally begin to write numbers with Roman figures, because the children of course will immediately understand them, and when you have got to the four you will easily be able, with the hand, to pass over to five — V. You will soon see that if you keep back your thumb you can use this four as the dog does!: I I I I. Now you add the thumb and make five — V.

I was once with a teacher who had got up to this point (in explaining the Roman figures) and could not see why it occurred to the Romans not to make five strokes next to one another but to make this sign V for the five. He got on quite well up to I I I I. Then I said: 'Now let us do it like this. Let us spread out our fingers and our thumb so that they go in two groups, and there we have it, V. Here we have the whole hand in the Roman five and this is how it actually originated. The whole hand is there within it.'

In a short lecture course of this kind it is only possible to explain the general principle, but in this way we can derive the idea of numbers from real life, and only when a number has thus been worked out straight from life should you try to introduce counting by letting the numbers follow each other. But the children should take an active part in it. Before you come to the point of saying, 'Now tell me the numbers in order, 1, 2, 3, 4, 5, 6, 7, 8, 9, and so on, you should start with a rhythm. Let us say we are going from 1 to 2, then it will be: 1, 2; 1, 2; 1, 2; let the child stamp on 2 and then on to 3 also in rhythm: 1, 2, 3; 1, 2, 3. In this way we bring rhythm into the series of numbers, and thereby too we foster the child's faculty of comprehending the thing as a whole. This is the natural way of teaching the children numbers, out of the reality of what numbers are.

Thus you must try to build up what the child has to learn as counting using a variety of approaches. And when you have worked in this way for a time it is important to pass on and not merely take counting by adding one thing to another; indeed this is the least important aspect of counting and you should now teach the child as follows: 'This is something that is ONE. Now you divide it like this, and you have something that is

TWO. It is not two ONEs put together but the two come out of the ONE.' And so on with three and four. Thus you can awaken the thought that the ONE is really the comprehensive thing that contains within itself the TWO, the THREE, the FOUR, and if you learn to count in the way indicated in the diagram, 1, 2, 3, 4 and so on, then the child will have concepts that are living and thereby come to experience something of what it is to be inwardly permeated with the element of number.

In the past, our modern conceptions of counting by placing one bean beside another or one bead beside another in the frame were quite unknown; in those days it was said that the unit was the largest, every two is only the half of it, and so on. So you come to understand the nature of counting by actually looking at external objects. You should develop the child's thinking by means of external things that can be seen, and keep as far away as possible from abstract ideas.

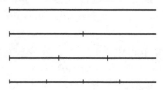

The children can then gradually learn the numbers up to a certain point; first, let us say, up to 20, then up to a hundred and so on. If you proceed on these lines you will be teaching them to count in a living way. I should like to emphasize that this method of counting, real counting, should be presented before the children learn to do sums. They ought to be familiar with this kind of counting before you go on to arithmetic.

Arithmetic too must be drawn out of life. The living thing is always a whole and must be presented as a whole first of all. It is wrong for children to have to put together a whole out of its parts, when they should be taught to look first at the whole and then divide this whole into its parts. Get them first to look at the whole and then divide it and split it up; this is the right path to a living conception.

Many of the effects of our materialistic age on the general culture of humankind pass unnoticed. Nowadays, for instance, no one is scandalized but regards it rather as a matter of course to let children play with boxes of bricks, and build things out of the single blocks. This of itself leads them away from what is living. There is no impulse in the child's nature to put together a whole out of parts. The child has many other needs and impulses that are, admittedly, much less convenient. If you give a child a watch for instance, the child's immediate desire is to pull it to pieces, to break up the whole into its parts, which is actually far more in accordance with human nature—to see how the whole arises out of its components.

This is something you should particularly bear in mind when teaching arithmetic. If you are walking towards a distant wood you first see the wood as a whole, and only when you come near to it do you perceive that it is made up of single trees.

This is just how you must proceed in arithmetic. You

never have in your purse, let us say, 1, 2, 3, 4, 5 coins, but you have a heap of coins. You have all five together, which is a whole. This is what you have first of all. And when you cook pea soup you do not have 1, 2, 3, 4, 5 or up to 30 or 40 peas, but you have one heap of peas. Or with a basket of apples, for instance, there are not 1, 2, 3, 4, 5, 6, 7 apples but one heap of apples in your basket. You have a whole. What does it matter, to begin with, how many you have? You simply have a heap of apples that you are now bringing home [*see diagram*]. There are, let us say, three children. You will not now divide them so that each gets the same, for perhaps one child is small, another big. You put your hand into the basket and give the bigger child a bigger handful, the smaller child a smaller handful; you divide your heap of apples into three parts.

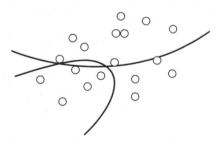

Dividing or sharing out is in any case such a strange business! There was once a mother who had a large piece of bread. She said to her little boy, Henry: 'Divide the bread, but you must divide it in a Christian way.' Then Henry said: 'What does that mean, divide it in a Christian way?' 'Well,' said his mother, 'You must cut the bread into two pieces, one larger and one smaller; then you must give the larger piece to your sister Anna and keep the smaller one for yourself.' Whereupon Henry said, 'Oh well, in that case let Anna divide it in a Christian way!'

Other conceptions must come to your aid here. We will do it like this, that we give this to one child, let us say [*see lines in the drawing*], and this heap to the second child, and this to the third. They have already learned to count, and so that we get a clear idea of the whole thing we will first count the whole heap. There are 18 apples. Now I have to count up what they each have. How many does the first child get? Five. How many does the second child get? Four. And the third? Nine. Thus I have started from the whole, from the heap of apples, and have divided it up into three parts.

Arithmetic is often taught by saying: 'You have 5, and here is 5 again and 8; count them together and you have 18.' Here you are going from the single thing to the whole, but this will give the child dead concepts. The child will not gain living concepts by this method. Proceed from the whole, from the 18, and divide it up into the addenda; that is how to teach addition.

Thus in your teaching you must not start with the single element to be added, but start with the sum, which is the whole, and divide it up into the single elements for adding. Then you can go on to show that it can be divided up differently, with different elements for adding, but the whole always remains the same. By taking addition in this way, not as is very often done by having first the elements for adding and then the sum, but by taking the sum first and then the elements for adding, you will arrive at conceptions that are living and mobile. You will also come to see that when it is only a question of a pure number the whole remains the same, but the single element for adding can change. This peculiarity of numbers, that you can think of the elements to be added as grouped in different ways, is very clearly brought out by this method.

From this you can proceed to show the children that when you have something that is not itself a pure number but that contains numbers within it, as the human being for example, then you cannot divide it up in all these different ways. Take the human trunk for instance and what is attached to it—head, two arms and hands, two feet. You cannot now divide up the whole as you please; you cannot say: now I will cut out one foot like this, or the hand like this, and so on, for it has already been structured by nature in a definite way. When this is not the case, and it is simply a question of pure counting, then I can divide things up in different ways.

Such methods as these will make it possible for you to bring life and a kind of living mobility into your work. All pedantry will disappear and you will see that something enters your teaching that the child badly needs. Humour comes into the teaching, not in a childish but in a healthy sense. And humour must find its place in teaching.[15]

11. Address at a Parents' Evening

Schools are now often referred to as learning communities and the phrase 'lifelong learning' is now a common concept. Steiner was clear that if these ideals were to have any reality it was a matter of practice and common endeavour for the sake of the child. A school is not formed for one generation alone and the adults in that community have to take on responsibilities and tasks that have long-term implications. Furthermore, without a strong parent-teacher relationship that was mutually supportive the educational philosophy he espoused would be less effective. This goes beyond conventional parents' evenings to the very governance and policies of the schools. The teachers' professionalism has to be respected as does the parents' wish to make a contribution with the skills and experience they bring with them. All want to serve a common purpose. At the time this was ground-breaking and even now it is a form of cooperation that is pioneering and experimental. The teachers are expected to form their cooperative work in such way that there is ongoing professional development; support and quality care practices are inbuilt into the daily life of the school. For the parents, with their daily responsibilities outside the school, it is more difficult to find a commonly acceptable form. In addressing these points so forcefully Steiner is posing a question for the future and, as so much in Steiner education, we have challenges to face with which we have barely begun. Yet at the same time the success of this approach is now well proven and over the years a body of experience has been accumulated that can be built upon. This requires a communal and selfless effort so that what is done becomes a 'social act of some consequence'.

Ladies and gentlemen! For a long time we have been aware of your active wish to have the issue of school and home, children and parents, discussed here at a parents' evening.

It is not possible to say everything there is to say on this subject in one evening, but we will continue to organize evenings where these questions can be discussed so that the topic can be covered exhaustively. Today I will articulate the basic main points that the teachers and I have in mind.

In the field of education, parents' evenings are often proposed, but many representatives, even outstanding ones, of today's official school system do not think much of such parents' evenings. Some excellent educators say that nothing comes of them except fruitless discussion. Now, different points of view are possible with regard to everything in practical life, including parents' evenings, and there is some foundation for all of them. I will not dispute people's right to think little of parents' meetings from their particular point of view. We, however, as representatives of the idea of the Waldorf school, must see something of extraordinary significance in these parents' evenings because, if these meetings can be conducted in the right way, they are connected to the conditions most necessary for the life of what we intend to bring about through the Waldorf school.

To be sure, teachers who have found their place in the social context that is prevalent today, who feel supported by state authorities, are at home and secure in this and are very often satisfied with it. There are plenty of people telling them what to do, so why take it from the parents too? This is how they look at it.

This cannot be our point of view. We are not embedded in current societal circumstances in the same way. We have to work on the basis of the guiding light of our understanding of human beings and of life, of human science and human art as our pedagogical goal. As educators, we must draw what we need for our teaching on a daily basis from the inner strength of our hearts. For that we need not recognition (an idea that derives as strongly as ours does from the challenges of the present and the future must be self-contained in the strength of its effectiveness and not count on recognition), but understanding — above all, the understanding of those on whom so much depends, of those who entrust their children to this school.

Without this understanding, we cannot carry out our work at all. This understanding must be general in nature at first. We cannot claim to be guided by a higher wisdom, derived from the acknowledged social order and hovering above our heads, and to need nothing more than awareness of this wisdom. We must gain leverage for the ideals of our school, and this happens when people see that what comes to light through the idea of the Waldorf school is very deeply rooted in the most important cultural demands of the present and the near future. Therefore, we must strive to present our intentions to our contemporaries in a clearly understandable form, in a form that can engender understanding. Above all, we count on the understanding of those who entrust their children to us, who therefore have a certain love for the Waldorf school. We count on them being able to grasp the thoughts, feelings and will impulses that sustain us.

Thus, we would like first and foremost to establish a relationship between the school and the parents that does not rest on faith in authority. That is of no value for us. The only thing that is of value is having our intentions received with understanding, right down into the details. The only thing that is of value is the awareness that this school is taking a great risk in trying to use feeble human forces to recognize the scarcely decipherable demands of the twentieth century and to recast them in the form of an educational venture. I believe there is no single member of our faculty who is not trying to experience what we are involved in as some kind of solid footing in world history, in humanity's evolution. This is what our teachers are trying to do in all modesty. As necessary as modesty may be, however, we must not be timid in what we are doing. We must be aware that what we are doing is significant, but also that this significance rests not in our own character but in what we acknowledge to be true. The significance of what we are doing must be looked at in the right way, not from an arbitrary or sympathetic standpoint, but from the standpoint of a will that stems from the awareness of the times. This, above all else, is what we need from the parents.

We would like the parents of the Waldorf school children to say, 'We are especially aware of our duty to educate human beings, and we would like to have our children make a contribution to humanity's great tasks in the twentieth century. We want entrusting our children to the Waldorf School to be a social act of some consequence.' The more strongly this becomes a part of your whole attitude, the better.

We have to depend on your attitude above all else. We cannot think much of detailed guidelines on how teachers are meant to act towards the parents and vice versa. We cannot expect much from these guidelines, but we can expect a great deal from meetings between teachers and parents that take place with the right attitude, because we know that when people's attitudes relate to their inmost being the attitude turns into action, right down into the details of life. When an attitude takes hold of a person on a general level, then his or her individual actions become copies of the broad strokes of the attitude's intentions. That is why it is more important for us to feel and understand the right thing in the right way than to lay down or follow specific guidelines.

I have emphasized how the different stages of life affect children, how children are different before the change of teeth from afterwards, in the period between the change of teeth and puberty. Up until the change of teeth, children's destinies actually keep them in very close contact with their parents and their home. If we are not totally caught up in the materialistic way of thinking that is flourishing at present, if we can see through to the spiritual context within human interactions and evolution, we know that the destined relationship between children and parents is much greater than our abstract age with its materialistic ideas often assumes. If in addition to knowing what physical life provides we know what is given to us by life in the spirit beyond the boundaries of birth and death, then we take the destined relationship between children, parents and siblings very seriously, and the way in which children come into elementary school from home, which is really incisive for all of education, acquires significance for us.

Although this first part of my remarks may be some-what far from the thoughts of most of you as parents, it still seems important to me to touch on this. Those of you who already have children with us may have younger children at home. You may have come to love the prin-ciples of the Waldorf school and want to send your younger children here too. For you, tonight's subject of raising pre-school children will be important.

On entering school, children are true reflections of all the characters and circumstances in their parent's home and in their environment as it has been until then. Up to the age of 7, children are almost entirely sense organ. They take in everything from their surroundings with incredible sensitivity—everything that is said, done and even thought. Hidden within this is a secret of human growth that is largely disregarded by today's science—expressions of soul in a child's surroundings are transformed into the child's organic, bodily constitution. Anyone who has acquired the educator's fine feeling for a child's appearance that a Waldorf teacher is meant to have will see by the shine in a new elementary school student's eyes whether that child has been treated lovingly at home or has been treated unlovingly and subjected to outbursts of anger in his or her environment. What parents and siblings and so forth do, say and think lives on in a child's bodily constitution. If I wanted to, I could say a lot about how these expressions of soul can be observed in the processes of breathing and blood circulation and in the working of the child's nervous system. Due to certain circumstances, the child's father and mother may tend to have frequent outbursts of anger in dealing with the child. In such children, we notice what they have taken in and bound up with their inner being. It has turned into their bodily constitution; it is there in how their digestion works, how their muscles move, and even in how they can and cannot learn.

It is literally, not figuratively, possible to say that when a first-grader is entrusted to a teacher, the teacher receives a complete image of the parents' home. In their health, temperament and ability to learn, children bring their home right into school. Our first intimate acquaintance with the home is through the child. This should become part of the attitude of those of us who have a real interest in schools such as the Waldorf school. Such things need only turn into an attitude to begin to affect our actions.

When you are clearly aware of something like this, you will do some individual things that you would otherwise not do and refrain from doing many things you would otherwise do. This is no abstract knowledge; it saturates your whole life. If this prerequisite is present, it will result in the will to bring parents and teachers together in the right way. When we know that what is important works in the depths of human nature, we pay less attention to what is actually said in words in five minutes, but much more to how it is said. When the attitude I indicated brings parents to school again and again to meet their child's teacher, the simple fact that parents and teachers are not strangers to each other but have seen each other before will start to bear fruit.

In this relationship between parents and teachers, what we need above all is for this interest in the generalities of Waldorf education to carry over to all aspects of school life, to everything that is connected to the Waldorf school through the faculty on the one hand and the parents on the other. If we know that at home there is a daily interest in what we as teachers are doing in the Waldorf School, then we can teach with a great feeling of reassurance, with a strength that gives us new incentives each day.

I do not deny the difficulty of mobilizing such interest. I am well aware that under current social conditions people have little time and energy to ask, 'How was it? What did you do?' when their children come home from school. I know that the children cannot expect their warm enthusiasm to elicit this question. The point is that parents should not ask this question out of a feeling of duty, but in a way that makes the children want to be asked. We should not be at all embarrassed that the children may sometimes tell us things that we ourselves have forgotten; that goes without saying and will pass unnoticed if the right enthusiasm is present on both sides. Do not underestimate this: if teachers can know that what they are doing sparks lively interest at home, if only for a few brief minutes, then they know that their work rests on a firm foundation. They can then work out of an atmosphere of soul that can have an inspiring educational effect on the children.

This is the most effective thing we can do to combat what has been termed by some of today's outstanding educators 'the war between parents and teachers'. That is what they call it when they are speaking among themselves. This war is a subject of secret discussion among many educators. It has led to a noteworthy expression that is becoming well known; young teachers in particular tend to use it: 'We have to start by educating the parents, especially the mothers.' We here, however, have neither the ambition nor sufficient Utopian sensibilities to do that. Not that we believe that parents are not educable or refuse to be educated, but rather because we want there to be a really intimate relationship of friendship between parents and teachers, a relationship based on the matter at hand. The parents' interest in the school can do a lot to bring this about.

While the parents' souls have very strong effects on their child's bodily constitution, it is only possible for teachers to work on the child's soul by means of soul resources. Here, in place of the imitative nature with which a child encounters his or her parents before the change of teeth begins, there appears the principle of a necessary and natural authority. This is something we must have, and teachers are especially supported in this if an interest such as I have described is present. Much of what the parents can contribute to supporting this authoritative strength, to enabling their child's teacher to be the authority that he or she must be, can have its source in something as simple as the fact that school is taken seriously, with a certain ceremonial seriousness. A lot of sifting out goes into choosing teachers for the Waldorf school, and they are people you can have confidence in. And if you do not understand something, rather than wrinkling your nose at it right away, it is important that you trust in the great overriding principle in which you yourself believe. Then you will be supporting your child's teacher and making use of the opportunity to bring about a relationship of trust between parents and faculty.

You know that we do not issue report cards with grades as the state schools do. Instead, we try to describe what is typical of each child and to enter into his or her individuality. First of all, if teachers sit down to formulate reports and are aware of the responsibility involved, then riddle upon riddle appears to their minds' eye, and they weigh up every word they write down. It is a great relief to them in this process if they have actually met the child's parents, not simply because this tells them about the family background, which is all materialism is concerned with today, but because it allows them to see the children's environment, and then everything begins to appear in the right light. It is not necessary for the teachers to judge the parents themselves in any indiscreet way; they simply want to meet the parents in a friendly manner. Just as writing a letter to someone you know is different from writing to a stranger, it is also different writing reports on students whose parents you know from those whose parents you have not met.

Secondly, the teacher should actually be able to know that such reports spark loving interest at home, and I believe that if parents would manage to write a brief response to what the teacher wrote in the report, it would be an incredible help. It would make no sense to institute this as a requirement, but it is extremely important from an educational standpoint if parents begin to feel the need to do this. Such notes are read with extreme attentiveness here in the Waldorf school. Even if they were full of mistakes, they would be much more important to us than many currently acknowledged accounts of modern culture. They would permit us to take a deep look into what we need if we are to teach, not out of abstract ideas, but out of the impulse of our times.

You must not forget that Waldorf teachers educate out of an understanding of the human being that does not come about in today's customary ways. A powerful human understanding would flow in what the parents could communicate to the teacher in a committed way, and I do not exaggerate at all when I say that a response to a report card would almost be more important for the teacher than the report itself is for the child.

Here too, however, I place more value on parents maintaining a lively interest in everything going on in the school than I do in this specific measure I have chosen as an example.

Thus it is my opinion that the right thing will happen in the time the children spend on vacation if the school year runs its course in the way I have indicated. We would do well to let the vacation be a vacation and not pin the children down to doing anything school-like. However, if you can make the attitude I wished for into a reality, that would mean the right kind of happiness, joy and healthy refreshment for your child.

We are particularly dependent on an atmosphere that is steeped in this attitude, so that you realize that the Waldorf teachers are concerned about every aspect of your child, including first and foremost his or her health. We are particularly concerned about being informed in our souls of subtleties with regard to the state of health of the children who are entrusted to us. An art of education is not complete unless it extends to this degree of interest in a child. This is an area, however, in which the work we need to do will be possible only if parents and school work together in the right way. We would like to see our school met by an understanding that arises from an inner need. We would also like to see the parents turn to the school for tips on their children's physical well-being, diet and so forth. Above all we want to see the fundamental impulse behind our activity in the school, namely, deep, inner human honesty and openness, take full effect in these details in the interaction between parents and teachers. This could lead to great results in life, and much could be done better in this regard if fathers or mothers came to the teachers and said, 'My children are coming home from school tired; they get home too late. What can I work out with you to counteract that?' Working things out in this frank way can be the basis for many good things to happen.

In particular, it can help the school a lot if the parents lend their support in things in which exactitude, but not pedantry, is needed. It contributes a lot to how we can maintain order in the school and create a mood of seriousness among the children if everything about how children and parents interact in the morning makes it a matter of course that the children leave the house at the right time and therefore arrive at school at the right time, without any special commands being issued. Here, too, it is not so much the individual instances I am referring to as the consciousness that stands behind them, the attitude that school is something serious and ceremonial and that when your teacher is satisfied with your punctuality, you satisfy your parents as well. This is a moral message that the children bring from home each morning. A child's state of mind on leaving the house in the morning is not merely a source of satisfaction or dissatisfaction to the teacher's educated eye. Disturbing or supportive impulses find their way into the teacher's mood, too, if the child leaves the house in one way rather than another. Such things need to become conscious. I believe it is of no small significance for the rest of your life to have heard as a small child from your father, 'There are two things that need to run exactly on time, you know—the clock, and getting children to school.' Saying that now and then does not take much time, but it will have an effect on the rest of your child's life.

We are not dependent on details, but rather on a heart-to-heart relationship between school and home. We are confident that if this real heart-to-heart relationship is present, the right thing will come of it. We long to see this attitude awakened not merely with regard to details, but in full force. Then the Waldorf school will accomplish something not only through its cultural consciousness but also through such things as we have discussed today.

We must be clear that in our times certain innovations have been necessary so that deficits in such things do not emerge too strongly. Just think of what kindergartens sometimes have to do to make up for what has been done badly at home! Our times have become such that they require surrogates for what should be experienced in the family.

What we are trying to accomplish in the Waldorf school is something that needs to be followed not only intellectually; it must also be loved. And if the parents' attitude is steeped in this love, we will not need to raise our children in fear and in hope, which are the two worst but most used means of educating children today. The best means of educating children, however, is and always has been love, and home can be a great support for a school whose art of education is sustained by love.

Some people say that the discipline in the Waldorf school is not as good as in other schools. Time is too short to speak about this in detail now. Simply keep in mind that things have changed a lot in recent years, not only in society but also in the souls of children. We cannot apply the standards of our own youth. There is a deep gap between the young generations of today and the older ones. And when getting an educational grasp on the being of a child is at issue, we will do badly if we educate on the basis of fear of punishment and hope for good grades, but we will do well if we teach out of love. No matter what kind of wild turmoil is going on in the classrooms, if children have the right relationship to their teachers, if the children are still able to see in their teachers what they are supposed to see, then all their boisterousness will not mean what it would mean otherwise. This may be paradoxical, but it is psychologically correct. We begin to look at boisterousness in a different way. The children are getting it out of their systems so that it will not have to come out later on, which is decidedly better than the other way around. Later stages of life are based on what we foster in school, you see. If we are deeply convinced that we are educating with a whole lifetime in mind and not just for the current moment, then we also know how much we need you parents in order to move forward with the idea of the Waldorf school.

These are the points of view I wanted to present first. I want to emphasize that they contain what is most important, and that we will get very far indeed by taking hold of them honestly and thoroughly. This will also strengthen the Waldorf teacher's sacred conviction, with which we hope you agree. We know that we will achieve our goal if the school's intentions are understood at home and if it is made possible for us to work together intimately with the parents.

12. Education in the Wider Social Context

One of the questions confronting Rudolf Steiner during the foundation of the first Waldorf school in 1919 was the relationship between education and the prevailing social order. He came to an agreement with the Württemberg authorities that the children would be able to transfer from class three to a maintained school seamlessly, because the same learning goals had been achieved in the Waldorf school. Similarly at the end of class six and eight. In turn, there was public funding for the school to ensure it really was accessible to all families who wanted their children to attend and, in the intervening years, the teachers would have complete freedom in the formation of the curriculum. The agreement stated, 'At the end of these stages the Waldorf school will have reached the same prescribed learning goals as the public schools.'

Naturally this particular arrangement might not be universally applicable now, as time and expectations have moved on, but it does show recognition of the realities of the world at the very inception of the school movement. An educator is expected to fight for what is considered right for the well-being of the child but must also be effective in achieving those ideals. Looking back on this in 1923, when a similar compromise had to be made for the Basle school, Steiner said in his lecture, 'What must never happen is to allow a more or less sectarian or fanatical zeal to creep into our educational endeavours, only to find at the end of the road that our pupils do not fit into life as it is. For life in the world takes no notice of one's educational ideals, but it is governed from the prevailing conditions themselves. Opponents of anthroposophy have often attributed fanaticism and sectarianism to this movement but, as you will see, these two attributes are alien to its nature.'[16] Dialogue and engagement with the world are vital if the children are not to be estranged from the world they will live in. As financial and economical structures are a part of our everyday life and influence us, however idealistic we may be, they too need to be reassessed in the light of progressive education. In this call for Inspiration, Imagination and Intuition Steiner is suggesting how this can be a constructive engagement and reinforce the attempt to produce a better and more harmonious social environment.

The child is only engaged by the picture if we ourselves believe in it. The genuine spiritual-scientific attitude should restore in us the faculty of seeing in nature not the ghostlike things of which science speaks, but the pictorial, the imaginative. What emerges from the chrysalis and is present in the butterfly is really an image of the immortality of the soul placed into the order of nature by the divine world order. If there were no immortal soul there would be no butterfly emerging from the chrysalis. There can be no real image if truth is not the basis for it. So it is with all of nature. What natural science offers is a ghost.

We can comprehend nature only if we know that it is an image for something else.

Likewise, people must accustom themselves to considering the human head as an image of a heavenly body. The human head is not round in order to resemble a head of cabbage, but rather to resemble the form of a celestial body. The whole of nature is pictorial and we must find our way into this imagery. Then there will radiate into the hearts, the souls and minds, even into the heads — and this is most difficult — what can permeate human beings they take in pictures. In the social organism we will have to speak with each other about things that are expressed in pictures. And people will have to believe in these pictures. Then from scientific circles people will come who are able to speak about the real place of commodities in life, because the commodity produced corresponds to a human need. No abstract concepts can grasp this human need in its social value. Only someone can know something about it whose soul has been permeated by the discernment that springs from imaginative thinking. Otherwise there will be no social development. You may employ in the social organism those who rightly ascertain what is needed, but if at the same time imaginative thinking is not incorporated in the social organism through education it is impossible to arrive at an organic social structure. That means we must speak in images. However strange it may sound to the socialist thinker of today, we must speak from human being to human being in pictures that induce imaginations in order to arrive at true social development. This indeed is how it must happen. The nature of a commodity will be understood at a feeling level by a science that acquires knowledge through pictures, and by no other science.

In the society of the future, a proper understanding of labour will have to be a dominating element. What people say today about labour is sheer nonsense, for human labour is not primarily concerned with the production of goods. Karl Marx calls commodities crystallized labour power. This is pure nonsense; because what happens when human beings work is that they use themselves up in a certain sense. Such self-consumption can be brought about in several ways. If you happen to have enough money in the bank or in your purse you can apply yourself in sport and use your working power in this way. You also might chop wood, or do some other chore. The work may be the same whether you chop wood or engage in a sport. The important thing is not the amount of work-power you exert, but the purpose for which you use it in social life. Labour as such has nothing to do with social life in so far as this social life is to produce goods or commodities. In the threefold social organism, therefore, an incentive to labour is needed which is completely different from the one that produces goods. Goods will be produced by labour because labour has to be used for something. But what must serve as the basis for a person's work is the joy and love for work itself. We shall only achieve a social structure for society if we find the methods for inducing human beings to want to work, so that it becomes natural for them, a matter of course, that they work.

This can only happen in a society that makes reference to inspired concepts. In future, people will not be motivated by joy and love for work — as was the case in the past when things were instinctive and atavistic — if society is not permeated by such ideas and feelings as enter the world through the inspiration of initiates. These ideas must carry people along in such a way that they have an awareness of the social organism and devote themselves to it. That is to say, work itself takes hold of their souls because they have an understanding of the social organism. Only those people will have such understanding who have heard and taken in those inspired concepts, that is to say, those imparted by spiritual science. We cannot use the hollow concepts proclaimed today if a love for work is to be reborn throughout humankind. We need spiritualized sciences that can permeate hearts and souls — permeate them in such a way that human beings will have joy and love for work. Labour will be placed alongside commodities in a society that not only learns about pictures through the educators of society but also hears of inspirations and such concepts as are necessary to provide the means of production and the necessary foundation upon which people can exist in our complicated society.

For this we further need to circulate intuitive concepts in society. The concepts about capital that you find in my book *The Threefold Social Order* will only flourish in a society that is receptive to intuitive concepts. That means: capital will find its rightful place when people acknowledge that Intuition must live in them; commodity will find its rightful place when the necessity for Imagination is acknowledged; and labour will find its rightful place when the necessity of Inspiration is acknowledged.

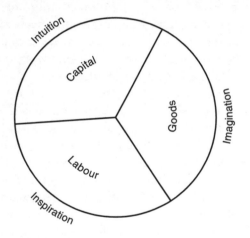

If you take the above diagram and do not write the three concepts one below the other but in the way I have done here, then you can learn a lot from it if you fill it with all the concepts to be found in my book about the threefold structure of the social organism. There are connections in both directions between labour and commodities and between commodities and capital, inasmuch as capital buys commodities, and there are connections between labour and capital, and so on. Only these three concepts must be arranged as shown.

Above everything, we must understand it is correct to say that in future the social order must become humanized. But it is necessary also to understand that the social order must be brought into being by people themselves; they must be willing to make up their minds to listen to the science of the initiates about imaginations, inspirations and intuitions. This is a serious matter, for by saying this I am stating nothing less than the fact that without the science of the spirit there will not take place in future any social transformation. That is the truth. It will never be possible to awaken in human beings the understanding necessary for matters like Intuition, Inspiration, Imagination, if you abandon the schools to the state. For what does the state make out of schools?

Just think of something which has eminently to do with both the school and the state. Think of civil rights, for example. These rights are supposed to arise in the sense of those practices people today consider the proper thing. Parliaments decide about civil rights (I am speaking of democracy, not monarchy). Civil rights are established through the representatives of everyone who has come of age. They are then incorporated in the body of law. Then the professor comes along and studies the law. Then he lectures on what he finds there as the declared civil rights. That is to say, the state at this point takes science in tow in the most deliberate way. The professor of civil rights may not lecture on anything but what is declared as rights in the state. Actually, the professor is not even needed, because one could record the state's laws, place a player on the speaker's desk and let it run. This then is science.

I am citing an extreme case. No one will seriously claim that the majority of decisions of parliaments today are inspired. The situation will have to be reversed. In spiritual life, in the universities, civil rights must come into existence as a science purely out of the human being's spiritual comprehension. The state can only attain its proper function if this is given to it by people. Some believe that the threefold structuring of the social organism aims to turn the world upside down. No, indeed. The world is already upside down; the threefold order wishes to put it the right way up. This is what is important.

We have to find our way into such concepts or we move towards mechanizing the spirit, falling asleep and vegetizing the soul, and animalizing the body.

It is very important that we instil in ourselves with the conviction that we have to think thus radically if there is to be hope for the future Above everything, it is necessary for people to realize that they will have to build the social organism upon its three healthy pillars. They will only learn the significance of Imagination in connection with commodities if economic life is developed in its pure form, and human beings are dependent upon conducting it out of brotherliness. The significance of Inspiration for labour, producing joy and love for work, will only be realized if one person joins another as an equal in parliaments, if real equality governs, that is, if every individual be permitted to contribute whatever of value lives in him. This will be different with each person. Then the life of rights will be governed by equality and will have to be inspired, not decided upon by the narrow-minded philistines as has been more and more the trend in ordinary democracy.

Capital can only be properly employed in the social organism if Intuition rises to freedom, and freedom blossoms from out of the independently developing life of the spirit. Then there will flow out of spiritual life into labour what has to flow into it. I will indicate the flows by arrows [*see diagram below*]. When organized in this way, these three spheres will interpenetrate one another in the right way.

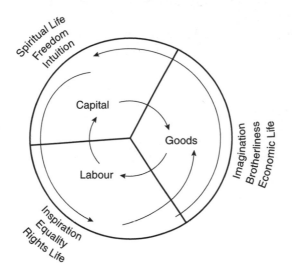

Now do not think this is an easy task. Many people believe today that they have already transformed their thoughts; they do not notice that they have retained the same old ones, especially in the field of education. Here you can have strange experiences. We tell people of the concepts spiritual science produces in the field of education. You may talk today to very advanced teachers, directors and superintendents of schools; they listen to you and say, 'Well, I thought that a long time ago; indeed, I am of exactly the same opinion.' In reality, however, they hold the very opposite opinion to what you tell them. They express the opposite opinion with the same words. In this way people pass each other by today. Words have lost connection with spirituality. It has to be found again or we cannot progress.

Social tasks, therefore, lie much more in the sphere of the soul than we ordinarily realize.

Afterword

by Christopher Clouder

The book *What's Worth Fighting for in Education* attempts to capture the passion and moral purpose that makes teaching worthwhile and thereby rebuild and redefine education. The authors begin by describing a contemporary phenomenon that is, in their view, affecting all schools.

> Beyond the walls of our schools the world is changing dramatically; and it is pushing and pressing down hard on those who work within. Rather than hiding from or shutting the classroom door on these external changes and developments, more and more teachers and head teachers are reaching out to people and organizations beyond the school — to parents, communities, businesses and the wider profession. They are searching for new and better ways to enrich, stimulate and support their own increasingly difficult and challenging work... These relationships ... must be emotionally rich and grounded in people's commitments to a shared moral purpose where the education of all children, not just the children in their own families or their own classrooms, matter most. Going wider with purpose

and integrity and emotional depth is imperative for teachers in many parts of the world now.[17]

These educational challenges are universal and not unique to any particular place or people, and are equally applicable to Steiner Waldorf schools. Yet the purpose, integrity and emotional depth that are required are not so readily available in our contemporary, competitive social world, and so the teacher must find new resources that rebuild and nourish these qualities. Patterns of social cohesion are also changing in many cultures and teachers are not impervious to these tendencies either. The lectures that Steiner gave on education make a deeply insightful and inspiring contribution to this debate, although they were given in the early decades of the last century.

One of the lessons of the last century is that the better we become at controlling the world of nature, the more difficult it is to maintain a humane social order. We have also become painfully aware that we have inclinations that can become visible in evil deeds. We have entered an age when such inclinations are present in all, and whether we commit evil deeds is dependent on something other than our inclinations. Steiner speaks of the necessity of developing a real vision of another person in the lecture *Evil and the Future of Man*. All art leads to deeper knowledge of humanity, and by entering into artistic forms we learn to comprehend other people pictorially. By learning to see through the picture nature of a human being we can gain a deeper vision of the other as an eternal being, and this we can perceive through our sense of warmth. We probably experience this more than we consciously acknowledge. He then suggests that we practise seeing through the veils of speech and language and try to perceive its inner gesture. Through art we can perceive the warmth in a fellow human being, through speech we can feel colour. These exercises enable us to understand one another across national, ethnic and cultural boundaries, and strive for the transmutation of evil.

In *Knowledge of the Higher Worlds*, Steiner describes the conditions needed for training one's higher abilities. One of them is to feel oneself a member of humanity as a whole and a true educator is someone who is constantly working on himself or herself:

Such an attitude gradually brings about a change in the whole of a man's way of thinking. This holds good in all things, the smallest and greatest alike. With this attitude of mind I shall see a criminal, for example, differently. I suspend my judgement and say to myself, I am a human being just as he is. The education which circumstances made possible for me may alone have saved me from this fate ... And then it will no longer be difficult for me to think that I am only a member of humanity as a whole and to share responsibility for everything that occurs. In such matters each one has to begin reforming oneself. It is of no avail to make general demands of humanity ...[18]

We face a twenty-first century reductionism, where our mentality is greatly influenced by an over-simplified evolutionary psychology, a middle class 'fear of failing', a persuasive neuro-science that proclaims that it is all in the brain and the mechanistic temptations of recombinant genetics. The powers of imagination, as exemplified in the adventures of *Alice in Wonderland*, where if she drank from a bottle marked 'Drink Me' she became very large — 'I know something interesting is sure to happen ... whenever I eat or drink anything' — and if she partook of a cake she became very small, have been replaced by the ubiquitous concept 'Buy Me' as an illusory panacea for all inner ills. Children are a ready market for this and can be cynically manipulated.

The extraordinary growth in information technology, with all its wizardry, provides us with untold sources of facts but no wisdom and no context or relationship for what it does supply. This we have to find for ourselves, and for this we need the life experience that children do not yet have. Computer technology contains the threat of standardized nurture instead of a preparation for ethical individualism and a loss of the personal interrelationships on which we thrive.

... many or most inventions were developed by people driven by curiosity or by a love of tinkering, in the absence of any initial demand for the product they had in mind. Once the device had been invented, the inventor had to find an application for it. Only after it had been in use for a considerable time did consumers feel that they 'needed' it . . . Thus invention is often the mother of necessity, rather than the other way round.[19]

Nobody decided a decade or so ago that children's educational progress would best be furthered by computers. Yet now they have become the long-sought answer, without any serious consideration of either their effects or how they could be used in a balanced way. They are a very useful tool and serve a part of our interest in the world, but they can also undermine our sense of a direct community and attack personal imaginative powers. That is not what Steiner meant by *interest*, and one limitation of computer technology is its incapacity to help us experience the warmth and the inner colour of each other. Healthy and innovative school communities can fill this gap and are increasingly called upon to do so. Social intelligence has become an important capability in turbulent social and technologically accelerated contexts.

In itself, 'intelligence' is an amazingly elastic word, a word that can cover multifarious concepts. In this context, Howard Gardner's book *Frames of Mind* (1983) is seminal, because for academic and educational circles it has liberated ideas of what intelligences are. The theory of multiple intelligences, although not the first suggestion of this sort in recent times, has opened up the debate and has provided a framework in which new and innovative educational ideas can be fruitfully discussed. The multi-faceted world of intelligence experienced by the ancient Greeks has been rediscovered in terms that are accessible and relevant for contemporary times.

In the last 30 years, there has been a reappraisal of older views of child development, for instance those of Vygotsky and Piaget. Researchers now basing their work on these great thinkers in the field of child development have found that children are much more intelligent than they were ever thought to be. Piaget said that young children had 'pre-causal thinking', but we now find that they do also have causal thinking. He said that children were ego-centric and saw the world only from their perspective and were greatly influenced by appearances. Research shows that this is not so, and that children have a very acute sensitivity to other people and can infer causes beyond appearance. I will give a short example related to me by an Early Years colleague. One day a girl of five, in a Waldorf kindergarten in England, came up to her teacher and she had scribbled on a page of a schoolbook a form of emergent writing. She then gave the book to the teacher and asked her to read it. The teacher, with creativity and fantasy, 'read' a story. The girl was very pleased. The next day, the girl came back and this time she had four pages of 'writing'. So once again the teacher did her best and turned it into a lovely story. Of course the following day the girl came back with even more pages. This time the teacher said she was sorry, she couldn't read it and she didn't have her glasses with her (which was, of course, true). She turned to the girl and said, 'Could you read it for me?' The girl immediately replied, 'No, I can't. It's in

French.' Who can say a 5-year-old is not intelligent? That is the Odysseus quality of creative thought that lives in our children so strongly and is too often unrecognized in our educational debates.

> On the basis of such data, I arrived at a firm intuition: human beings are better thought of as possessing a number of relatively independent faculties, rather than having a certain amount of intellectual horsepower, or IQ, that can simply be channelled in one direction or another. I decided to search for a better formulation of human intelligence. I define an intelligence as a psycho-biological potential to solve problems or to fashion products that are valued in at least one cultural context.[20]

Gardner's definition of intelligence is closely linked to brain research and, at that time, he defined seven abilities that met his criteria. He now proposes nine, having later identified a 'naturalist' intelligence whereby we recognize and categorize natural objects, as well as a possible 'existential' intelligence, which captures and ponders the fundamental questions of existence. In his basic definition the Greek link between doing and thinking is accentuated: '...to solve problems and to fashion products'. His point of departure is that such a capacity must be psycho-biological. In other words, he will not define anything as an intelligence unless evidence for it can be found in the brain itself. Further, he says that all human beings are intelligent, and that this is a basic definition of humanity, but that no two human beings have the same intelligence—none of us have the same combination of intelligences. He then goes on to suggest that these intelligences are connected; they are not separate streams. So, for instance, he talks about 'the Mozart effect', whereby, through music, one can enhance one's spatial intelligence. This has been taken up in the educational debate of late as a more competitive academic curriculum threatens artistic and creative elements in schools. Music is important in the development of young children, both for their thinking and spatial capacities, and what they learn and experience in this field is transferred into abilities in other forms of intelligence. Would we have the theory of relativity if Einstein had not played the violin? The arts as such are therefore an essential foundation in any Steiner school, not a luxury that can be discarded because of other pressures.

Gardner states in his earlier works that intelligence should not be conflated with values. We use values to try and understand what intelligence is and we define intelligence by our values, but it is not values. Because we know something is wrong, through our capacity of intelligence, it does not mean we are not going to do it. Motivation is something that can be differentiated. In the quality or state of being motivated, there is something that goes beyond intelligence. Gardner takes this theme up in his latest book, *The Disciplined Mind—What all Students Should Understand*, where he explores the combination of values and intelligence. He says the following:

I am convinced that much of the dis-ease found in our society, at a time when it appears in some ways to be as 'successful' as it has ever been, comes from these troubling disjunctions. We observe daily that only one kind of talent — say technological creativity — is being rewarded and only one measure — say profit in the market place — is being recognized. Yet we know in our bones that these indices are insufficient, that other parts of the human spirit ought to command recognition, respect and veneration. A person can succeed on Wall Street or in Washington and yet fail as a human being. To be sure, it would be more difficult, more controversial, to agree on what embodies these 'soft' virtues and these 'connections'. And yet, as a society, we do not feel legitimate unless we make the effort to do so... We are born as little creatures, and for years we feel relatively helpless. And of course, a feeling of insignificance is appropriately part of our human condition. We live for but an instant, and even for that instant, there are billions of other, equally worthy, human beings on the face of this tiny planet.

During our moment, however, we should try to make the most of our vantage point. Education can equip us to make a difference, and perhaps it can orientate us towards making a positive one. We must be humble in the face of biological limitations under which we operate. We must be equally humble with reference to the constraints and opportunities afforded by the culture in which we happen to be born and those to which we are exposed by our schooling, our travel, our media, and our personal contacts.

Our contributions depend on our rootedness in visions of the true, the beautiful and the good; our willingness to act upon these visions individually and synergistically; our understanding of the changes as well as the constants in the world; and the accident of our location in a particular domain, institution or problem space at a particular historical moment.[21]

This is a direct reiteration of the basis of the curriculum of a Steiner school in a contemporary idiom and mindset.

This is also an argument for pluralism and one can find a similar plea in Goleman's book *Emotional Intelligence*. Gardner argues for pluralism; there must be different schools for different children, with different curricula to meet the different needs of the moment because there is not one single incontrovertible truth, beauty or morality. Yet these are the very concerns that in his view should animate education. Different schools should have different curricula so that children can approach different topics along different routes. In other words, human differences and intelligences should be recognized and accommodated educationally. He supports Goleman to the extent that he agrees that empathy is part of emotional intelligence but insists it should not be confused with intelligence. For his part, Goleman suggests that Gardner is only concerned with how thoughts affect feelings and ignores how feelings affect thoughts. Yet even in their disagreement, the need for a more pluralistic approach to education is manifested.

> Being able to put aside one's self-centred focus and impulses has social benefits; it opens the way to empathy, to real listening, to taking another person's perspective. Empathy, as we have seen, leads to caring, altruism and compassion. Seeing things from another person's perspective breaks down biased stereotypes, and so breeds tolerance and acceptance of differences. These capacities are ever more called on in our increasingly pluralistic society, allowing people to live together in mutual respect and creating the possibility of productive public discourse. These are the basic arts of democracy.[22]

In *Pedagogy of the Oppressed*, Paulo Freire distinguishes two types of educational practice. One he calls the banking concept of education, the other is the problem-posing method. In the banking form, the educator cognizes a cognizable object as he prepares his lesson and then expounds on that subject to the students. They are not expected to know but just to memorize. The problem-posing approach does not have this dichotomy where the teacher moves between cognitive and narrative. She is cognitive both in preparation and with the students. What is cognized is not viewed as private property, but lives as the object of reflection by herself and the students. The gesture is one of giving. In other words, the students are not listeners but co-investigators in dialogue with a teacher who constantly re-forms her reflections. There is a joint responsibility for the process. 'Problem-posing education affirms men and women as beings in the process of becoming—as unfinished, uncompleted beings in and with likewise unfinished reality ... the unfinished character of human beings and the transformational character of reality necessitate that education is an ongoing activity.' The child can actively participate in the reflective aspect out of which the teacher also grows. As Steiner pointed out, in the last analysis there is no curriculum as such, only teachers and children, and a living education is what exists in their relationship with each other. Teaching is a learning profession and one in which taking care of children's development has to have a practical aspect as well as an idealistic foundation.

> The moral agent in the ethics of care stands with both feet in the real world ... The care ethicist sees this precisely as a crucial condition for being able to judge well ... The ethics of care demand reflection on the best course of action in specific circumstances and the best way to express and interpret moral problems. Situatedness in concrete social practices is not seen as a threat to independent judgement. On the contrary, it is assumed that it is exactly what will raise the quality of judgement.[23]

Education is about change and therein lies its difficulty. Nothing stands still and yet we all need some ideas and ideals onto which we can hold. Steiner's achievement was to acknowledge and study the transformative nature of the human spirit and bring that into a practical and effective reality within an educational environment. His lectures inspired many people during his lifetime and close study of their content can also show new ways forward for what is becoming an increasingly valuable and demanding vocation. Our children deserve the best we can offer them, as the challenges ahead are likely to be more complex and morally demanding than those of the present. An education based on insights into a humane anthropology and a recognition of spiritual realities, however difficult it might be to measure up to, is essential.

Notes

1 Handy, C., *The Empty Raincoat*, Arrow Books, 1995.
2 See Walafrid's introduction to Einhard's *Vita Karoli*. In: Thorpe, Lewis G.M., *Two Lives of Charlemagne*, Penguin Classics, 1969, p. 49.
3 Elkind, D., in Waldorf Education Research Institute *Research Bulletin*, Vol. 13, No. 1, 1998.
4 Steiner, R., *Unzeitgemäßes zur Gymnasialreform*, 1898, GA 31, p. 232.
5 Steiner, R., *The Education of the Child*, Anthroposophic Press, 1996, p. 20.
6 Delors, J., et al., *Learning, The Treasure Within*, UNESCO, 1998, p. 58.
7 Gardner, H., *The Disciplined Mind*, Simon & Schuster, 1999, p. 251.
8 Steiner, R., *Education as a Social Question*, Anthroposophic Press, 1969, p. 106.
9 Ibid.
10 Steiner's words as reported by Herbert Hahn, the first teacher appointed to the new school.
11 Sacks, O., 'Neurology and the Soul', *New York Review*, 12/11, 1990, p. 44.
12 See Rudolf Steiner, *Soul Economy and Waldorf Education*, Rudolf Steiner Press, 1986.
13 Donaldson, F., 'Nothing Special in the Company of Children'. In: *The Future of Childhood*, Hawthorn Press, 2000, p. 133.

14   Rex Raab, 'Obituary for Erica Baravalle', in *Lehrerrundbrief*, 53, 99.

15   At this point Dr Steiner turned to the translator and said: 'Please be sure you translate the word "humour" properly, for it is always misunderstood in connection with teaching!'

16   Steiner, R., *The Child's Changing Consciousness*, Anthroposophic Press, 1988, p. 150.

17   A. Hargreaves & M. Fullan, *What's Worth Fighting for in Education*, Open University Press, 1968, p. 1.

18   Steiner, R., *Knowledge of the Higher Worlds*, Rudolf Steiner Press, 1973, p. 108.

19   Jarish Diamond, *Guns, Germs and Steel*, Vintage, 1998, p. 242.

20   Gardner, H., 'A Multiplicity of Intelligences', *Scientific American*, Vol. 4, No. 9, Winter 1998, p. 20.

21   Gardner, H., *The Disciplined Mind*, Simon & Schuster, NY, 1999, pp. 250–51.

22   Goleman, D., *Emotional Intelligence. Why it can matter more than IQ*, Bloomsbury, London, 1996, p. 93.

23   Sevenhuijsen, Selma, in *Beyond Early Childhood and Care*, ed. Moss, P., OECD Conference, Stockholm 2001.

Sources

Chapter 1
A Social Basis for Education, Stuttgart, 18 May 1919
In: *A Social Basis for Education*, Steiner Schools Fellowship Publications, 1994, pp. 19–25 (GA 192)

Chapter 2
The Spirit of the Waldorf School, Stuttgart, 31 August 1919
In: *The Spirit of the Waldorf School*, Anthroposophic Press, 1995, pp. 44–51 (GA 297)

Chapter 3
Educational Methods Based on Anthroposophy, Oslo, 24 November 1921
In: *Waldorf Education and Anthroposophy*, Vol. 1, Anthroposophic Press, 1995, pp. 173–98 (GA 304)

Chapter 4
The Child at Play, Basle, 10 May 1920
In: *The Renewal of Education*, Steiner Schools Fellowship Publications, pp. 166–73 (GA 301)

Chapter 5
Teaching from a Foundation of Spiritual Insight, Berlin, 14 May 1906
In: *The Education of the Child and Early Lectures*, Anthroposophic Press, 1996, pp. 41–8 (GA 96)

Education in the Light of Spiritual Science, Cologne, 1 December 1906
In: *The Education of the Child and Early Lectures*, Anthroposophic Press, 1996, pp. 52–62 (GA 55)

Chapter 6
The Adolescent after the Fourteenth Year, Dornach, 4 January 1922
In: *Soul Economy and Waldorf Education*, Rudolf Steiner Press 1986, pp. 224–32 (GA 303)

Chapter 7
Science, Art, Religion and Morality, Ilkley, 5 August 1923
In: *A Modern Art of Education*, Rudolf Steiner Press, 1972, pp. 24–37 (GA 307)

Chapter 8
The Spiritual Ground of Education, Oxford, 22 August 1922
In: *Spiritual Ground of Education*, Anthroposophical Publishing Company 1947, pp. 55–60 (GA 305)

Chapter 9
The Role of Caring in Education, Lecture 6, Dornach, 20 April 1923
The Child's Changing Consciousness, Anthroposophic Press, 1988, pp. 127–37 (GA 306)

Chapter 10
The Roots of Education, Bern, 15 April 1924
The Roots of Education, Rudolf Steiner Press, 1982, Lecture 3, pp. 59–65 (GA 309)

The Kingdom of Childhood, Torquay, 16 August 1924
The Kingdom of Childhood, Anthroposophic Press, 1995, Lecture 5,
pp. 72–82 (GA 311)

Chapter 11
Address at a Parents' Evening, 22 June 1923
Rudolf Steiner in the Waldorf School, Anthroposophic Press, 1996,
pp. 119–202 (GA 298)

Chapter 12
Education in the Wider Social Context, Lecture 3, Dornach, 11
August 1919
Education as a Social Problem, Anthroposophic Press, NY 1969,
pp. 54–63 (GA 296)

Further Reading

Introductions to Steiner education

C. Clouder & M. Rawson, *Waldorf Education*, Floris Books, 1998

F. Carlgren, *Education Towards Freedom*, Lanthorn Press, 1972

Early years

S. Jenkinson, *The Genius of Play*, Hawthorn Press, 2001

L. Oldfield, *Free to Learn*, Hawthorn Press, 2002

B. Patterson & P. Bradley, *Beyond the Rainbow Bridge,* Michaelmas Press, 2000

Class teaching

T. Finser, *School as a Journey*, Anthroposophic Press, 1994

Upper school

B. Staley, *Between Form and Freedom*, Hawthorn Press, 1998

C. Clouder & D. Mitchell (eds.), *Rudolf Steiner's Observations on Adolescence*, Association of Waldorf Schools in North America, 2001

Curriculum

A. Nobel, *Educating Through Art*, Floris Books, 1996

C. Lindenberg, *Teaching History*, Association of Waldorf Schools in North America, 1991

J. Kiersch, *Language Teaching*, Steiner Schools Fellowship Publications, 1997

M. Rawson & B. Masters (eds.), *Towards Creative Teaching*, Steiner Schools Fellowship Publications, 1996

Anthroposophy

S. Easton, *Man and World in the Light of Anthroposophy*, Anthroposophic Press, 1975

Note Regarding Rudolf Steiner's Lectures

The lectures and addresses contained in this volume have been translated from the German, which is based on stenographic and other recorded texts that were in most cases never seen or revised by the lecturer. Hence, due to human errors in hearing and transcription, they may contain mistakes and faulty passages. Every effort has been made to ensure that this is not the case. Some of the lectures were given to audiences more familiar with anthroposophy; these are the so-called 'private' or 'members' lectures. Other lectures, like the written works, were intended for the general public. The difference between these, as Rudolf Steiner indicates in his *Autobiography*, is twofold. On the one hand, the members' lectures take for granted a background in and commitment to anthroposophy; in the public lectures this was not the case. At the same time, the members' lectures address the concerns and dilemmas of the members, while the public work speaks directly out of Steiner's own understanding of universal needs. Nevertheless, as Rudolf Steiner stresses: 'Nothing was ever said that was not solely the result of my direct experience of the growing content of anthroposophy. There was never any question of concessions to the prejudices and preferences of the members. Whoever reads these privately printed lectures can take them to represent anthroposophy in the fullest sense. Thus it was possible without hesitation — when the complaints in this direction became too persistent — to depart from the custom of circulating this material "For members only". But it must be borne in mind that faulty passages do occur in these reports not revised by myself.' Earlier in the same chapter, he states: 'Had I been able to correct them [the private lectures], the restriction *for members only* would have been unnecessary from the beginning.'

The original German editions on which this text is based were published by Rudolf Steiner Verlag, Dornach, Switzerland in the collected edition (*Gesamtausgabe*, 'GA') of Rudolf Steiner's work. All publications are edited by the Rudolf Steiner Nachlassverwaltung (estate), which wholly owns both Rudolf Steiner Verlag and the Rudolf Steiner Archive. The organization relies solely on donations to continue its activity.

For further information please contact:

Rudolf Steiner Archiv
Postfach 135
CH-4143 Dornach

or:

www.rudolf-steiner.com

AGRICULTURE

Compiled with an introduction, commentary and notes by
Richard Thornton Smith

The evolving human being; Cosmos as the source of life; Plants
and the living earth; Farms and the realms of nature; Bringing
the chemical element to life; Soil and the world of spirit;
Supporting and regulating life processes; Spirits of the elements;
Nutrition and vitality; Responsibility for the future

ISBN 1 85584 113 4

ARCHITECTURE

Compiled with an introduction, commentary and notes by
Andrew Beard

The origins and nature of architecture; The formative influence
of architectural forms; The history of architecture in the light of
mankind's spiritual evolution; A new architecture as a means of
uniting with spiritual forces; Art and architecture as
manifestations of spiritual realities; Metamorphosis in
architecture; Aspects of a new architecture; Rudolf Steiner on the
first Goetheanum building; The second Goetheanum building;
The architecture of a community in Dornach; The temple is the
human being; The restoration of the lost temple

ISBN 1 85584 123 1

ART

Compiled with an introduction, commentary and notes by
Anne Stockton

The being of the arts; Goethe as the founder of a new science of
aesthetics; Technology and art; At the turn of each new
millennium; The task of modern art and architecture; The living
walls; The glass windows; Colour on the walls; Form — moving
the circle; The seven planetary capitals of the first Goetheanum;
The model and the statue 'The Representative of Man'; Colour
and faces; Physiognomies

ISBN 1 85584 138 X

MEDICINE

Compiled with an introduction, commentary and notes by
Dr Andrew Maendl

Understanding man's true nature as a basis for medical practice;
The science of knowing; The mission of reverence; The four
temperaments; The bridge between universal spirituality and the
physical; The constellation of the supersensible bodies; The
invisible human within us: the pathology underlying therapy;
Cancer and mistletoe, and aspects of psychiatry; Case history
questions: diagnosis and therapy; Anthroposophical medicine in
practice: three case histories

ISBN 1 85584 133 9

RELIGION

Compiled with an introduction, commentary and notes by
Andrew Welburn

Mysticism and beyond: the importance of prayer; The meaning
of sin and grace; Rediscovering the Bible; What is true
communion?; Rediscovering the festivals and the life of the
earth; Finding one's destiny: walking with Christ; The
significance of religion in life and death; Christ's second coming:
the truth for our time; Universal religion: the meaning of love

ISBN 1 85584 128 2

SCIENCE

Compiled with an introduction, commentary and notes by
Howard Smith

From pre-science to science; The origin of mathematics; The roots
of physics and chemistry, and the urge to experiment; Are there
limits to what science can know?; Understanding organisms:
Goethe's method; The quest for archetypal phenomena; Light,
darkness and colour; The rediscovery of the elements; What is
warmth?; The scale of nature; The working of the ethers in the
physical; Sub-nature; What are atoms?; Natural science and
spiritual science

ISBN 1 85584 108 8

SOCIAL AND POLITICAL SCIENCE

Compiled with an introduction, commentary and notes by
Stephen E. Usher

Psychological cognition; The social question; The social question
and theosophy; Memoranda of 1917; The metamorphosis of
intelligence; Culture, law and economy;
Central Europe between East and West

ISBN 1 85584 103 7